# FINDING
# JESUS

A 21-day devotional designed to help people overcome addiction by fasting while learning about Jesus.

## Christopher Ozbirn

Published by Inscript Books
a division of Dove Christian Publishers
P.O. Box 611
Bladensburg, MD 20710-0611
www.inscriptpublishing.com

Inscript and the portrayal of a pen with script are trademarks of Dove Christian Publishers.

Book Design by Mark Yearnings

ISBN: 978-1-957497-04-4

Published in the United States of America

# Contents

# How to Use this Devotional

This devotional aims to help you identify any possible areas of addiction in your life. If you find yourself struggling with life, then you are not alone. I have been there myself. For 25 years, I was lost in addiction, spending most of my life alone in a virtual world. I created this devotional to help you examine yourself and reveal any addictions that you may have. This way, you can identify the problem, address it, and remove it from your life.

The other purpose of this devotional is to lead you to an encounter with Jesus, the one who can help you overcome any area of addiction you may find, as well as any other struggles. You can use this devotional, even if you don't believe in Jesus. My goal isn't to force you to believe anything. Rather, it is to help you learn more about who Jesus really is and why He can help you through your struggles and addictions. Then you can decide whether to change your views about Jesus. This decision is entirely up to you.

The first thing I am asking you to do is pick a substance, activity, or behavior in your life that may be causing problems. I explain how to do this on day one. Fast from that substance, activity, or behavior for 21 days while following this devotional. Fast simply means stop doing it. If you are unsure what to start fasting from, days one, two, and three of this devotional are designed to help you figure this out.

The reading for each day consists of four parts. The first part of each day is a question followed by an answer based on my personal experience or what the Bible says about it. I have asked myself each of these questions during the process of seeking Jesus to overcome my addiction.

In the second part of each day, you should ask yourself the following self-reflection questions:

1. Are you feeling more anxious, angry, or irritable than normal during this time of fasting?
2. Are you having trouble focusing on normal activities during your fast?
3. Are you counting down the days until your fast ends?
4. Are you feeling a strong desire to break your fast?
5. Is taking time away from your substance, behavior, or activity easy or hard?
   a. On a scale of 1 to 10, how would you rate the difficulty, with 10 being the hardest?
6. Do you feel like you have lost something important to you during this fast?
7. Are you having difficulty wanting to engage in other activities?
8. Is your fast affecting your relationships in a better way or a worse way?
9. Do you feel bored, like you have nothing to do during your fast?
10. Do you have other activities that you enjoy doing?
    a. Can you do those with others?
    b. How does doing these activities make you feel?
11. When you are reading the Bible and learning about Jesus, how does that make you feel?
    a. Do you enjoy it?
    b. What are you learning about Jesus or the nature and character of God?

These questions are designed to help you think about how fasting from this substance, activity, or behavior makes you feel. You have to be completely honest with yourself here.

For the best results, I suggest reading these questions at

the beginning of each day to give you an idea of what you should be thinking about. At the end of each day, reread them and write down your answers based on how you felt that day. As you go through this fasting period, these answers may change. That's OK as long as you are being honest with yourself.

The third part of each day will be a personalized prayer for you to pray based on what you learned during the discussion question. You are welcome to make this prayer more personal in any way you feel you need to. As I was developing this program, this is what I felt that I should be praying myself.

When praying, find a quiet place where there are no distractions. Kneel and recite the prayer with all your heart and mean it. Cry out to God and ask Him for help. He wants to hear from you.

The last part of each day will be a reading assignment from *The Gospel According to John*. Read the chapter for the day in the Bible if you have one. If not, you can go to this website: www.bible.com/bible/100/JHN.1.NASB1995 or download any free Bible app on your app store. I personally like the YouVersion Bible app, but any app will do. You can read any translation of the Bible you feel comfortable with. The three I use most are the New American Standard Bible (NASB), The Amplified Bible (AMP), and the New King James Version (NKJV). Next, answer the questions to help you comprehend what you are reading. If you don't know how to answer these questions, don't worry; just keep reading the chapter in John daily and keep going.

I have designed this devotional to be read and studied with someone else. It could be another person struggling with addiction, a friend or family member, a pastor, a therapist, or a faithful believer in Jesus who can help you learn. Share with each other daily about how you feel based on the self-reflection questions. Go over the Bible study questions together to help you both grow to know Jesus more intimately.

The last thing I suggest is to start going to a local church every Sunday if you aren't already attending a church. Pray to God to help guide you where to go. Then start attending churches in your area until you find the one the Spirit leads you to regularly attend. Being a part of a local church will help you learn more about Jesus from a pastor who is called to preach. Also, having a pastor to answer questions you may have during this process would be very helpful.

# Finding Jesus Worship Song Playlist

I have created a playlist of worship songs to listen to each day. I believe each song speaks to something learned during that day's lesson. Each song is available on YouTube.

Day 1. "Start Right Here" by Casting Crowns
Day 2. "Dead Man Walking" by Jeremy Camp
Day 3. "God turn it around" by Jon Reddick
Day 4. "So Long Self" by Mercy Me
Day 5. "So Will I (100 Billion X)" by Hillsong UNITED and Benjamin Hastings
Day 6. "I'm Sorry" by Toby Mac
Day 7. "Jesus Messiah" by Chris Tomlin
Day 8. "Redeemed" by Big Daddy Weave
Day 9. "Let Go, Let God" by Jack Cassidy
Day 10. "More of You" by Colton Dixon
Day 11. "Holy Spirit" by Bryan & Katie Torwalt
Day 12. "What You Want" by Tenth Avenue North
Day 13. "If We're Honest" by Francesca Battistelli
Day 14. "The Proof of Your Love" by for KING & COUNTRY
Day 15. "Hello, My Name is" by Matthew West
Day 16. "Confidence" by Sanctus Real
Day 17. "We All Need Jesus" by Danny Gokey & Koryn Hawthorne
Day 18. "Gotta Tell Somebody" by Don Francisco
Day 19. "Never Going Back" by Skillet
Day 20. "Chain Breaker" by Zach Williams
Day 21. "God I Look to You" by Bethel Music and Francesca Battistelli

# Introduction

*Hi, my name is Chris. I am a faithful follower of Jesus Christ. I am a video game addict.*

This is the introduction I was taught to do during my first ever experience with a twelve-step recovery program. It was a Christ-centered program that dealt with any difficulties life could throw at you, from drug addiction to divorce, surviving abuse, co-dependency, and anything in-between. But I want to be honest with you; I haven't always been a faithful follower of Jesus. I wasn't delivered from my addiction in a twelve-step program. But this program gave me the support I needed to learn how to live after my addiction. So let me start from the beginning.

I was raised in a broken home from the time I was seven years old. Neither of my parents had a close personal relationship with Jesus. They were both looking for love, which they needed from Jesus, in relationships. They never truly found that love in their relationships. When I was 23 or 24, they finally stopped looking. They had been married and divorced a total of eight times between them. This was a pattern of behavior I would repeat myself later in life. I am sure it is no surprise after hearing this that I have had a skewed view of what love is for most of my life.

My dad introduced me to video games shortly after my parent's divorce. I really enjoyed playing them as a child. But I also enjoyed doing other things like riding my bike outside and playing basketball. At this time of my life, video games were something I enjoyed but not something I was addicted to. Later in life, that would change.

My mom's third husband, Jimmy, started abusing me sexually around the age of 10 for two years. During this time of abuse, video games went from a form of entertainment to a coping mechanism I used to survive my abuse. After my abuse, I began to rely more and more on video games to escape other problems in my life.

Around 12, I finally found the courage to tell my dad about the abuse. He pressed charges against Jimmy. After a year and a half of therapy, I testified against Jimmy. He was convicted and just finished a sentence of 27 years.

After I reported my abuse, my dad and grandmother started taking me to church. It was there that I first heard about Jesus. I learned that He died on the cross for me, and His death would save me from my sins. I also learned that I shouldn't keep on sinning.

While I had gained knowledge of Jesus, no one explained how to be a committed, lifelong learner and follower of Jesus or a disciple of Jesus. The process of helping someone learn how to be a disciple of Jesus so that they can go out to help others grow more spiritually mature is called disciple-making. I didn't have anyone at that time to teach me disciple-making.

In Matthew 13:20-21, Jesus explains the parable of the sower who sowed his seed on rocky ground. Jesus said, *"The one on whom seed was sown on the rocky places, this is the man who hears the word and immediately receives it with joy; yet he has no firm root in himself, but is only temporary, and when affliction or persecution arises because of the word, immediately he falls away."*

Because I had only heard of Jesus and not truly experienced Him personally, affliction would come later in life, and I would walk away from my faith as the prodigal son did in another of Jesus' parables.[1]

By 26, I had already followed my parent's example. I had already married and divorced twice. During this time, I was introduced to massively multiplayer online role-playing games. My game of choice at the time was *World of War-*

*craft*. It was an online fantasy game where you had to work with other players to achieve a common goal. This game temporarily gave me a sense of purpose and met my needs for companionship during my singleness. I would date off and on, and I met my third wife within three years.

We dated for a year, conceived a child, and then got married. Like I said before, I wasn't living a lifestyle that followed God's design. Two days after our wedding, I received a call from my second wife. I was informed that she would be moving my youngest daughter into the home of her boyfriend's brother, a convicted sex offender. Two days later, we were in court filing for temporary emergency custody of my daughter.

This was the beginning of a downhill spiral of difficulties that would last for the first five years of our marriage. Needless to say, I started running away from my problems into this fantasy gaming world every chance I got. I now had a full-blown addiction.

During the eight years of our marriage, my wife would repeatedly tell me that I needed to back off my video games. I was playing way too much, not helping her as much as she felt I should, and neglecting her and my children. Time and time again, I would tell her I would. I would try for a little while and fall back into my addiction. I can't tell you exactly how many times this happened. It was at least eight, but it could have been many more. As much as I loved my wife and my children, I was trapped in a prison of my mind that I couldn't escape. No matter how hard I tried, my desire to escape my problems by gaming trumped any rational judgment I attempted to have. I didn't know the way out.

For at least seven years of our marriage, my wife and I regularly attended church. And while attending church, I wasn't personally seeking to know Jesus in my daily life. My pastor did a good job explaining what a personal relationship with Jesus should look like. There was no one-on-one discipleship training, nor was there any accountability at all. If discipleship training programs and accountability were available, I wasn't aware of them nor wanted to seek them.

But I had an interest in learning about Jesus. I would speak with my father-in-law, a pastor, about Jesus and a co-worker who was a strong Christian woman. They were the closest things in my life I had to what a disciple-maker should be.

In 2018, the pastor of my church challenged us to a church-wide fast starting sometime in January. I had not really heard of fasting before. But the pastor explained that a fast isn't necessarily about food. You can choose anything to fast from that keeps you from seeking Jesus. I immediately knew what I would have to fast from—my video games. I thank Jesus for giving me this insight.

My father-in-law had bought me a book on Revelation that I had asked for Christmas. I started the fast early before the rest of the church did, stopped playing my video games during this time, and started reading this book. While I was reading, I heard the Holy Spirit speak to me. He said plainly, "Why are you reading about the end of my life when you don't know me from the beginning?" I have since learned that when Jesus speaks to you in the Spirit, you listen.

What the Spirit said to me made sense. I set my mind to reading the gospels of Matthew, Mark, Luke, and John. Then I would start re-reading my book on Revelation. What I didn't know was that Jesus had other plans for me. Jeremiah 29:11 (NIV) says, *"'For I know the plans that I have for you,' declares the Lord, 'plans to prosper you and not to harm you, plans to give you hope and a future.'"*

As I was meeting Jesus for the first time in my life at the age of 38, I felt a fire light inside of me. This person that I had heard about my whole life was actually real. And He loved me! I learned that He loved me so much that He gave His life up for me! [2] It wasn't just some story I heard in church. Or a fairytale. Jesus was ALIVE! And He wanted to know ME personally.

The fasting period for the church was supposed to last 21 days. I fasted from sometime early January until middle to late March. During this time, I read the whole New Testament, thoroughly read the book I had on Revelation, and dieted, resulting in the loss of 30 pounds. I can't explain it, but it seemed so easy for me at the time. The only thing I was doing differently was fasting and spending time with Jesus by reading His Word. Doing these things helped me rely on Jesus' power through the Holy Spirit He placed in me, instead of relying on my own power.

Even though I had this wonderful and miraculous experience with Jesus, I still wasn't ready to submit it all to Jesus. I was still holding tightly to one thing: my addiction to video games. In March 2018, I stopped fasting and started playing my video games again. It didn't take long for it to consume me again.

Sometime in early May, my wife again, for the umpteenth time, told me that I was getting too deep into my gaming, and I needed to back off. I told her I would, as usual. I work the night shift at a local hospital, seven days on, seven off. A couple of weeks after I had told my wife I would back off gaming, I had taken four extra days off, giving me eleven days off in a row instead of my typical seven. During the first half of my time off, I did well, staying away from my video games and paying attention to my wife and children. I was attempting to do this by my own power, so I fell right back into my addiction. And this time, I was all-in. I was completely neglecting my wife and kids. I saw a change in my wife's behavior during this time. But I was so focused on my gaming, I couldn't even take time to ask her what was wrong. Sound familiar?

When I went back to work that Friday night, the Jesus I had met personally earlier that year had something to say to me about my behavior. The Holy Spirit in me said, "Son, you saw a change in your wife's behavior, and you were powerless to do anything about it. You have to stop your gaming now!"

Jesus revealed the truth that I wasn't willing to admit to myself. John 14:6 says, *"Jesus said to him, 'I am the way, and the truth, and the life; no one comes to the Father but through me.'"*

After He said this to me, He showed me how much my video game addiction had hurt my wife, children, friends, and family. He also revealed how much time I had lost that I could have been serving Jesus for the Kingdom of God. I felt immediate conviction and cried out to Jesus. I repented when I got home from work that morning. I deleted the app from my phone that I had been playing.

When I woke up that afternoon, I went to my wife, ready to repent and tell her the good news. 1 John 1:9 says, *"If we confess our sins, He is faithful and righteous to forgive us our sins and to cleanse us from all unrighteousness."*

Little did I know, the good news for me wasn't good news for her. You see, I wasn't trustworthy. I had lied, deceived, and manipulated her for over eight years so that I could spend more time playing video games. When I told her the news, she thought I was lying to her again. She had news for me as well. She was done with the marriage. She wanted a divorce.

My heart was broken. I was devastated. I played Russian roulette with my marriage one too many times. And this time, the gun was loaded, ready to go off. I didn't understand why she couldn't give me one more chance to show her I was serious this time. Looking back, now I do. I didn't deserve her trust.

Why am I giving you this personal testimony about my life? While I may have lost my marriage, I had finally found the courage to fully submit my life to Jesus, this time including my video game addiction. The reason why I was able to get to this point was because I spent almost three months fasting while getting to know Jesus in a personal way through reading the Bible.

Listen to what is said in the book of Isaiah 58:6, *"Is this not the fast which I choose, to loosen the bonds of wickedness, to undo the bands of the yoke, and to let the oppressed go free and break every yoke?"* Fasting and seeking Jesus led me to the personal encounter with Jesus I needed to help me know the truth about myself.

I truly believe had I not committed that time fasting and reading the Bible, I would still be a lost addict to this day. Jesus wouldn't save me from the consequences of my choices, but He did save me from eternal separation from Him in hell.

I want to share this same gift with you. A personal experience with Jesus. I want to help you evaluate your life to determine whether or not there is something that you are holding on to keeping you from seeking Jesus. I truly believe that fasting, daily Bible reading, guided self-examination, and someone who cares about you to help you through this process will help you have the same breakthrough in your life that Jesus provided for me.

# Day 1: How Does the World Define Addiction?

As I started serving in a local ministry helping the homeless, I met Chris Payne. Chris started a ministry called A WAY OUT. His ministry helps people dealing with addictions or other struggles in life by sharing his testimony that Jesus is our only way out. When I met him and heard his message, I knew that he truly knew Jesus. I knew he had a heart for loving others where they were and leading them to Jesus. And I wanted to help him serve others. His testimony resonated with me.

In his testimony, Chris tells people that nobody ever told him about Jesus when he struggled with his addiction. Nobody shared the gospel with him or told him that Jesus loved him and wanted to help him. I felt the same way.

Nobody told me that playing video games excessively was an addiction. Nobody told me that I needed help and that help was in the person of Jesus. If someone sat me down and explained that I was using my video games as a way of escape and running from my problems into this fantasy world, I may have been willing to listen. I was running away from Jesus, the only one who could help me heal from my past hurt.

This is why I wrote this book for you. To tell you the truth. Jesus said to his disciples in John 8:31-32, *"If you abide in My word, you are truly my disciples. And you will know the truth, and the truth will set you free."*

Remember, as I said before, Jesus is the truth. It makes sense to me now why fasting and studying the Bible, which is Jesus' word, helped set me free from my addiction. I am telling you the truth, that getting to know Jesus will set you free.

In high school, math was my favorite subject. I took every math class that was offered, from geometry to calculus. Math is about problem-solving using numbers. How does that relate to addiction? Before you can find a solution to a problem, you first have to define the problem. We know the problem we are addressing in this book is addiction. Then what is addiction?

The Merriam-Webster Dictionary[1] defines the word *addiction* in a couple of ways. First, addiction is defined as "a compulsive, chronic, physiological or psychological need for a habit-forming substance, behavior or activity having harmful physical, psychological or social effects and typically causing well-defined symptoms such as anxiety, irritability, tremors or nausea upon withdrawal or abstinence." That's a lot to take in. Let's break it down bit by bit.

Let's take a look at this phrase first, "a compulsive, chronic, physiological or psychological need." *Compulsive* means something that you feel drawn to do without giving it much thought. *Chronic* means it lasts for an extended period or is ongoing. A *physiological* need is something that meets your body's physical needs. And finally, a *psychological* need is something that is meeting a need in your mind. This phrase, put more simply, is this: I am drawn to do something without thinking about it repeatedly over a long period of time that is meeting a need of my body or my mind, maybe even both. Now let's look at the next part of the definition.

The next part, "need for a habit-forming substance, behavior or activity," defines the need we are discussing in the first phrase. The word *habit-forming* is a key word here.

In simple terms, it means behavior that we start doing that becomes hard to stop doing. This means we develop a need for a substance, behavior, or activity that is hard to stop doing. The usual thing we would think about here would be smoking, drinking, or using drugs. This is only a small part of the definition.

It also includes behaviors and activities. Take a break and reflect a few minutes on habitual behaviors or activities that you may be doing that may be included in this part of the definition. A few examples that come to mind would be watching TV, spending time on Facebook, watching You-Tube, playing a video game, or any other activity you may be doing without giving it much thought. Think of some behaviors or activities that may apply to you and write them down for future reference.

The next part of the definition states: "having harmful physical, psychological or social effects." This part is pretty straightforward to understand. This substance, behavior, or activity has not only become habitual but is causing us harm in a physical, psychological, or social way.

When I was spending so much time playing video games, I didn't have a very active lifestyle. Sometimes, I would also spend the time sedentary, snacking, or eating foods that weren't always healthy. This caused me to gain weight. That is an example of a physical effect. Other physical effects include insomnia, weight gain or loss, increased heart rate, or high blood pressure.

Let's look at an example of a psychological effect now. When I was addicted to video games, I was using video games as a way of escaping the pain and struggles I was facing. Using video games as a coping mechanism to escape pain instead of facing problems and overcoming them is an example of a psychological effect.

Other psychological effects of addiction include cravings, a decrease in pleasure in everyday life, and being in denial when someone addresses your behavior as hurtful or damaging to them. These are some but not all psychological effects of addiction.

What about social effects? What does that look like? I spent most of my time playing video games while I was home with my wife and children. How much time I spent playing video games versus how much quality time I spent with my wife and children caused a social effect. I was spending all of the quality time I had playing video games, and my wife didn't like that very much. Although I was always there with her next to me, in reality, my mind was in a virtual world. She felt alone most of the time we were together. I honestly can't tell you how often she told me she thought I cared more about playing video games than I did for her. This activity had a social effect on my wife and our relationship.

Other social effects of addiction can include interference with normal daily activities such as work, school, relationships, and household chores, and it can cause financial difficulties due to excessively spending money on your addiction. Communication issues were a big issue for me as well. It was hard to have healthy conversations with people because I didn't have anything in common with them to talk about. I also didn't want to spend time talking or paying attention to anyone because it would take time away from playing my video games.

Now, take a few minutes to reflect on the list you made earlier. Do the things on your list affect your life physically, psychologically, or socially? If so, take a few minutes to write examples of how these things affect your life. Although this may be hard for you to do, share what you have written down with the person you are reading this devotional with or someone close to you. Ask them a question:

"Do you think these possible areas of addiction in my life are affecting my life physically, psychologically, or socially?" Be ready to receive an honest answer.

Let's look at the last part of the phrase; "typically causing well-defined symptoms such as anxiety, irritability, tremors or nausea upon withdrawal or abstinence." This part of the phrase determines whether you have a bad habit or a full-blown addiction. Ask yourself whether fasting from the substance, behavior, or activity causes you to have any psychological symptoms, such as anxiety or irritability, or physical symptoms, such as nausea or tremors. If so, then you may have an addiction. These are just examples of what can happen. There are many more symptoms.

When you define any problem areas you may have, you can start looking for solutions. Knowing the problem can give you hope that the solution is coming soon. Tomorrow, we will discuss the second definition of addiction in detail. We will be asking, "How does God define addiction?"

> *Before proceeding to the next section, review and ask yourself the self-reflection questions listed in the "How to Use This Devotional" section at the beginning of this book.*

# Day 1 Prayer:

Father God, I am starting a journey with Your Son, Jesus. I am learning about who He is and seeking to learn some things about myself that I may not like to find out. I need You to help me. Help me be honest with myself about who You are. Also, help me be honest with myself about any substances, activities, or behaviors in my life that may not be pleasing to You. Search me thoroughly, O God, and know my heart; test me and know my anxious thoughts, see if there is any wicked or hurtful way in me, and lead me in the everlasting way. Tell me the truth about whether or not I have an addiction in my life that is keeping me from seeking to know You, Father. Show me how my activities may be hurting myself or those around me. Lead me into admitting those things to myself, so I can learn how to let go of those substances, actions, or behaviors that cause me pain. I cannot do this alone, Father; I need You to walk me through it. I am asking You in Jesus' Mighty Name, Amen.

# Day 1 Bible Study Questions

Read John chapter 1 and answer the following questions:

1. In John 1:1-5, what person is John describing as the Word?
2. What qualities does this person exhibit?
3. What did this person do in the beginning? Refer to Genesis 1:1, Isaiah 9:6, John 8:12.
4. Who was John the Baptist?
5. What was his role given to him by God?
6. How did his role fulfill an earlier prophecy? Refer to Matthew 3:1-17; Mark 1:1-13, Luke 3:1-22, Malachi 3:1,
7. Who was Jesus?
8. What was He sent to do for us?
9. Who were the people called to follow Jesus?
10. Who did they say Jesus was?

# Day 2: How Does God Define Addiction?

God sees addiction in a much different light. I will start with the second definition of addiction in the Merriam-Webster dictionary. Then I will explain what the Bible says about this definition. After that, I will show how the Bible says we can overcome our addiction.

The second definition of addiction in the Merriam-Webster dictionary is "a strong inclination to do, to use, or to indulge in something repeatedly." [1] It is a much simpler definition than the first. What does the word *inclination* mean? It has four definitions, according to the Merriam-Webster dictionary. [2]

First, *inclination* is defined as "a tendency to a particular aspect, state, character or action." Second, *inclination* is defined as "a deviation from the true vertical or horizontal." Third, *inclination* is defined as "an act or the action of bending or inclining." *Bowing* is what comes to mind. Last, *inclination* is defined as "a particular disposition of mind or character." I can see how all four of these definitions can be applied to addiction.

First, I want to focus on the third definition of inclination. It is "an act or the action of bending or inclining." We know the Bible doesn't specifically mention addiction, but what does it say about inclining? I am glad you asked.

The first time the word *incline* is mentioned in the Bible is in Joshua 24:23. It says, *"Now therefore, put away the foreign gods which are in your midst, and incline your hearts to the Lord, the God of Israel."* Two things are going on here. First, Joshua is telling the people of Israel to put away the foreign gods, or idols, in their midst. Why is this important?

The first two commandments God gave Moses are found in Exodus 20:3-4. He said, *"You shall have no other gods before Me. You shall not make for yourself an idol, or any likeness of what is in heaven above or on the earth beneath or in the water under the earth. You shall not worship them or serve them; for I, the Lord your God, am a jealous God."*

They had already broken God's first two commandments by creating idols and worshipping them instead of God. Take a moment or two and ask yourself, "Am I worshipping God first in my life? Or am I worshipping something else? How much time am I spending seeking a personal relationship with God? How much time am I spending doing activities other than seeking a personal relationship with God? Is participating in these other activities keeping me from drawing closer to God?"

The second thing Joshua said in verse 23 was, *"Incline your hearts to the Lord, the God of Israel."* It is reasonable to assume that the inclination of our hearts and what we worship are related. Look at what Solomon said in Proverbs 2:2, *"Make your ear attentive to wisdom, incline your heart to understanding."* Solomon also said in 1 Kings 8:57-58, *"May the Lord our God be with us, as He was with our fathers; may He not leave us or forsake us, that He may incline our hearts to Himself, to walk in all His ways and to keep His commandments and His statutes and His ordinances, which He commanded our fathers."* That's twice that Solomon connected inclination to the heart.

We are to incline our hearts to the Lord. If we incline our hearts to anything other than the Lord, in His eyes, we are worshipping that before Him. We are making it an idol. We have already established that addiction and inclination are closely related. God sees addiction as the sin of idolatry.

In the other definition I will discuss, inclination is "to deviate from the true vertical or horizontal." What did Jesus say the greatest commandment was? Vertical love for God, horizontal love for one another. [3] To deviate from this is to fall outside of God's design.

Proverbs 4:25-27 says, *"Let your eyes look directly ahead, and let your gaze be fixed straight in front of you. Watch the path of your feet, and all your ways will be established. Do not turn to the right nor to the left; turn your foot from evil."* God wants us to walk a path that is straight and narrow. Think of a line. When you deviate from a line, you get a hill or a valley. That's what addiction is, highs and lows, which lead to more highs and lows in an endless cycle until it is broken. How do we break the cycle? By following Jesus.

In Matthew 4:19, Jesus told his disciples, *"Follow Me, and I will make you fishers of men."* Then Jesus took them and showed them what that looked like. Matthew 4:23 says, *"And Jesus went about all Galilee, teaching in their synagogues, preaching the gospel of the kingdom, and healing all kinds of sickness and all kinds of disease among the people."* Addiction is a sickness that needs to be healed. Jesus healed sick people. Therefore, we need Jesus to heal us, and we need others to help support our healing along the way.

From this point forward, I will be referring to addiction as idolatry, the way God sees it. Unless I say otherwise, if I mention idolatry, I am referring to addiction. How do we stop our idolatry? God tells us how to stop worshipping our idols in Isaiah 30:18-22. Here's what it says:

*18 "Therefore the Lord longs to be gracious to you, and therefore He waits on high to have compassion on you. For the Lord is a God of justice; How blessed are all those who long for Him.*

*19 O people in Zion, inhabitant in Jerusalem, you will weep no longer. He will surely be gracious to you at the sound of your cry; when He hears it, He will answer you.*

*20 Although the Lord has given you bread of privation and water of oppression, He, your Teacher will no longer hide Himself, but your eyes will behold your Teacher.*

*21 And your ears will hear a word behind you, "This is the way, walk in it," whenever you turn to the right or to the left.*

*22 And you will defile your graven images, overlaid with silver, and your molten images plated with gold. You will scatter them as an impure thing; and say to them, "Be gone!"*

When I prayed and asked God to show me how to help people overcome their idolatry, God showed me these verses. But He also gave me a message. He told me, "This is the key that unlocks the door." I didn't understand what He meant at first. But He showed me an example.

Imagine someone lost in idolatry is trapped in a locked room and doesn't know how to get out. Anyone who is truly dealing with idolatry knows what I am talking about. How do they get out if they don't have the key? They need someone to help them by bringing them the key. The key to escape is a relationship with Jesus; the door that leads out is the door to salvation.

Now let's break down the verses in Isaiah 30:18-22 line by line so I can give you the key. In verse 18, the Hebrew word for the verb longs is *ḥāḵâ*. It means "to actively wait expecting a result." [4] For God, this means He is actively waiting above for us to come to Him so that He can be gracious to us and give us His compassion. For us, it means God wants us to actively wait for Him and expect His best during difficult times.

What does God's graciousness look like? In Hebrew, the word for gracious is *ḥēn*. It means "leaning towards. This refers to the Lord's favor, out of His kind disposition, leaning towards people to bless them." [5] What does God's compassion mean? The Hebrew word for compassion, *rāḥam*, comes from the root word that means *womb*. It shows how God is "intimately attached to us and showing tender concern towards us like a mother towards her child." [6]

Think about this for a minute. I want it to sink in. God is in Heaven, while we are sinning against Him in idolatry. He is actively waiting to bless us out of His goodness and loves us intimately like a mother loves her child. And He wants us to long for Him in the same way. When we do that, He will bless us.

How will He bless us? In verse 19, it says that when we face difficulties in life and cry out to Him in distress and a deep sense of desperation, He will be gracious to us and answer our cries. Verse 20 says that although He has allowed us to suffer trials and difficulties, after we have cried out to Him, He will reveal Himself to us, and we will see Him.

Verse 21 is an amazing verse to me. Jesus is with us, right behind us, whispering in our ears, guiding us in the way that we should go. You can't get more intimate than that. This shows how much Jesus loves us.

Now imagine how a mother leads her toddler child in a line. She stands behind the child, guiding him with her hands when he veers off to the right or left. But she allows the child to believe that he is leading himself. That is what Jesus does for us in verse 21 after we long for Him and cry out to Him.

In verse 22, God shows us how we overcome our idolatry. We cast it away from ourselves. This happens because of what it says in verses 18 through 21. When we set our hearts to long for the Lord and cry out to Him in need because of the troubles our idolatry has caused us, He hears us and reveals Himself to us. He then guides us back to the straight path He wants for us. And because we now know our God, we no longer need our idols, so we destroy them ourselves out of our love for Him.

I have personally experienced Isaiah 30 in my life. This truth of how I overcame my idolatry through fasting and seeking a relationship with Jesus perfectly aligned with Isaiah 30:18-22. I felt compelled to share this with anyone willing to listen. This experience God gave me is why I decided to write this book. I want others to overcome their idolatry through fasting and seeking Jesus.

> *Before proceeding to the next section, review and ask yourself the self-reflection questions listed in the "How to Use This Devotional" section at the beginning of this book.*

# Day 2 Prayer

Father God, today You have shown me how You see addiction. You call it idolatry. Father, search my heart and reveal to me if I am worshipping anything in my life other than You. "Give ear to my prayer, O God; And do not hide Yourself from my supplication. Give heed to me and answer me; I am restless in my complaint and am surely distracted, because of the voice of the enemy, because of the pressure of the wicked; for they bring down trouble upon me, and in anger they bear a grudge against me." [7] "But You, O Lord, are a shield about me, My glory, and the One who lifts my head. I am crying out to You Lord with my voice, and You will answer me from Your holy mountain." [8] Thank you, Father, for longing for me and waiting for me to realize that I need You. I do need You, Father; I want to long for You. Help me with that. I cry out to You in my need; I need You to help me destroy my idols. Whisper in my ear, O Lord; guide me to Your straight and narrow way. I ask You all these things and give You all the glory, honor, and praise, Father. In Jesus' Mighty Name, I pray, Amen!

# Day 2 Bible Study Questions

Read John Chapter 2 and answer the following questions:

1. Why did Jesus turn the water into wine?
2. What did that act reveal about who Jesus was?
3. What were the people doing in the temple area that made Jesus angry?
4. What did Jesus do about it?
5. What did Jesus mean when He says, "destroy the temple and I will rebuild it in three days?"

# Day 3: Am I Consuming Entertainment, or is Entertainment Consuming Me?

One of the goals of this book is to help people recognize any idols that may exist in their hearts. When we identify the idol, we can address it directly and learn how to properly give our hearts to Jesus. The question we will consider is: Am I consuming entertainment, or is entertainment consuming me? Answering this question will help us examine our lives and hearts to see if any form of entertainment has become an idol.

Before I get into the thick of explaining what this question really means, let me be honest with you. I don't believe in asking anything of anyone that I haven't or wouldn't ask of myself. That is called hypocrisy. God hates a hypocrite. Read about Jesus, and you will see that. I want to share some of my testimony to show you how I addressed this issue.

For most of my adult life, I can honestly say that my idolatry of video games consumed me. I would spend eight or more hours per day playing video games multiple times per week. I would do this instead of spending quality time with my wife and children. I had no friends at that time nor any desire to make a friend. Being a friend requires an investment of your time. And that would take away time that I could be playing video games.

As I was fasting, I had to really examine my life. I had to ask myself hard questions like the one I am asking you to answer for yourself. When I answered those questions, I had to face the truth. I had a problem, and I needed a solution.

Thankfully, when asking these questions, I also sought a closer relationship with Jesus. Without knowing it, I was given the way to heal my problem of idolatry: a relationship with Jesus. I wanted to share this with you because I want you to see that I am not asking these questions to judge you myself because I am in no place to judge. Instead, I want to offer you a solution to a problem I had to face.

Back to the question: Am I consuming entertainment, or is entertainment consuming me? First, I want to explore the meaning of the words used in the question. This will help us fully understand what we are asking ourselves. Then, I want to talk about different types of entertainment that have become idols for us and why this is true. Then, I want to discuss what God says about consuming entertainment. Lastly, I want to offer you some questions to ask yourself so you can start searching your heart like I did.

First, I want to define the word *consume*. The Merriam-Webster dictionary defines *consume* in the following ways: The first is "to do away completely, or destroy." The second is "to spend wastefully, or squander; to use up." The third is "to eat or drink especially in great quantity; to enjoy avidly, or devour." The fourth is "to engage fully, or engross." The fifth is "to utilize as a customer." [1]

Each definition of *consume* lists it as a transitive verb, requiring a direct object. In other words, you ask *what* or *whom* after the verb used. What am I consuming? The answer is entertainment. Who is entertainment consuming? The answer is me. In our question, this is the proper usage and definition for the word *consume*.

Now let's define *entertainment*. Merriam-Webster defines *entertainment* in two ways. The first is "amusement or diversion provided especially by performers." The second is "something diverting or engaging." [2] The word *diversion* is included in both definitions. What is the purpose of the diversion? What are the people creating the entertainment trying to divert us from or toward?

Before we seek to answer these new questions, let's return to our original question in light of the definitions of the words *consume* and *entertainment*. Am I consuming entertainment? The word *consume* is used mostly as a negative term meaning to squander, destroy, devour, or engross. Any of these words would make the point, but I want to focus on the word *destroy*.

Let's ask the question using the word *destroy* in place of *consume*. Am I destroying entertainment, or is entertainment destroying me? Asking the question in this context changes how we look at the answer.

You may be asking, "How can entertainment destroy me?" That's a good question; let's look at the definition of entertainment. It means something diverting or engaging. Is entertainment diverting your attention from seeking a daily relationship with Jesus? Yesterday, we discussed that anything you choose to put before God is an idol. If your answer is yes, I want to ask the question from that context.

The question now becomes, "Am I destroying my idols, or are my idols destroying me?" Yesterday, we redefined addiction from a Biblical perspective. We decided to call any addiction that we have an idol or idolatry. Remember this fact: when entertainment goes from something we occasionally enjoy to something we are constantly doing, it becomes an idol for us because it diverts us from spending time seeking Jesus.

Now that we have properly defined the question from God's perspective, let's discuss the types of entertainment that may be idols for us. They include:

- Social media.
- Video games.
- Watching video entertainment in all forms, including YouTube, TV shows, movies, and short video clips like TikTok.
- Anything else you do to entertain yourself that keeps you from seeking Jesus.

I want to discuss in more detail how social media and video games are specifically made to keep you coming back.

If you are spending more time than you should using social media, you are not alone. According to Statista, "people worldwide spend an average of 147 minutes a day using social media." [3] This is just an average based on polling. Most people probably don't realize how long they use social media daily. Why do people feel the need to use it in the first place?

According to Dr. Billi Gordon in an article published in Psychology Today, "The Ventral Tegmental Area (VTA) of the brain monitors social needs by releasing dopamine when we achieve social success and inspiring neurochemical deficits when we don't." [4] What does this mean for social media users? When we get likes on our posts or obtain followers, our brain releases dopamine.

What does this dopamine do for us? According to Dr. Susan Weinschenk in another article published in Psychology Today, "You may have heard that dopamine controls the 'pleasure' systems of the brain; that dopamine makes you feel pleasure and therefore motivates you to seek out certain behaviors, such as food, sex, and drugs. Recent research is changing this view. Instead of dopamine causing you to experience pleasure, the latest research shows that dopamine causes seeking behavior. Dopamine causes you to want, desire, seek out, and search. It increases your general level of arousal and your goal-directed behavior." [5]

What does this mean for social media users? Every time we get a like on a post, obtain followers, or other social media approval, dopamine is released in our brains, causing us to seek more approval and attention to get another dopamine release. This leads one to seek social media approval more than anything else, possibly creating an idol in our lives. This isn't necessarily bad news, though. Taking a break from social media can restore your normal brain chemistry. This is one of the reasons I am promoting a period of fasting to determine if you have an area of idolatry in your life.

Now let's look at video games. Why do we play video games in the first place? What about video games keeps us coming back? What needs do we have that video games are meeting?

Video games give us a sense of freedom and purpose, and some provide a social connection. When playing a video game, you aren't confined to the same rules we have in society. I was playing video games to escape from facing any difficulties in life. Playing video games also gives us purpose when we complete a level, achieve a goal, or defeat a boss. What I found most addictive was the social aspect of gaming.

When I discovered online games, I met people who had similar interests as I did. In real life, at the time, I didn't know anyone who played video games. It was hard for me to talk to people because all I knew was gaming. But in online gaming, I met people who understood what I liked and wanted to do it with me. That gave me a sense of purpose as well as community.

The biggest problem that kept me coming back was that I felt needed by others. In online games, there are tasks or bosses that you can't defeat alone. That is by design. Game designers appeal to our desire to feel needed and exploit it to keep us playing their game.

Remember the game *World of Warcraft* that really started my addiction? It was first released in 2004. Would you be surprised that 18 years later, it is still an active game with active players? This is a true statement. There are players that started in 2004 that are still playing to this very day. Think about that for a moment. People have invested over 18 years of their life into a virtual world. I was one of those people. The question we must ask ourselves is, "Why?"

The answer is simple. The game is meeting their needs. They have friends that they play with. They have spent hundreds, if not thousands, of hours making their virtual character strong to achieve the game's goals. And for me, I had my identity tied to the character I was playing. If these people enjoy what they are doing and do not hurt anyone in the process, why is this a bad thing?

This is the question that can be harder to answer. It is different for every individual, depending on their individual circumstances. But there is one common truth no matter a person's circumstances. If they spend all of this time playing a video game and not seeking a relationship with Jesus, it is an idol for them.

My friend, Opie Hurst, is a Christian counselor who led me down the path of writing this book. He posed a question to me the other day. He asked, "Why does someone want something so bad that they are willing to sin to get it?" The reason he asked this question is because sin has eternal consequences. If we die in sin, not believing in Jesus, we will spend eternity in hell, separated from God. This entertainment in our lives is keeping us distracted from that truth. Now we can look at the real question from God's point of view. "Am I destroying my idols, or are my idols destroying me?"

God's existence isn't dependent on our belief in Him. We only exist because God exists. That is the absolute truth we will face one day, whether or not we want to. Am I destroying my idols, or are my idols destroying me? What does God say in the Bible about this?

Joshua 24:20 says, *"If you forsake the Lord and serve foreign gods (idols), then He will turn and do you harm and consume you after He has done good to you."* This is an excellent example of how God uses the word *consume* in the context of idolatry. Let's take a look at what the word *consume* means to God.

The word used in this verse for consume is *kālâ*. It means "to be complete or to reach the end point of a process either for good, like God's perfect, finished work, or destruction, completely 'moved off the scene.'; the end, where there is no more to do; 'utter end,' like total destruction, or full purity," [6] depending on whether or not you have put your faith in Jesus.

In the context of Joshua 24:20, God will destroy you because you rejected His commandment to not serve any other god before Him or create any idols [7]. Psalms 145:20 says, *"The Lord keeps all who love Him; but all the wicked, He will destroy."*

The one sure thing I can tell you is that throughout the Old Testament, God never falters when it comes to someone worshipping an idol before Him. That is the one sin that God won't forgive you for if you don't repent and turn to Him.

Solomon was the wisest man in the Bible. He wrote the books of Proverbs, Ecclesiastes, Lamentations, and Song of Solomon. He was the king of Israel that God used to build the first temple for Him. He had all that he could ever want in life, but this is what he wrote later in Ecclesiastes 2:10-11: *"And all that my eyes desired I did not refuse them. I did not withhold my heart from any pleasure, for my heart was pleased because of all my labor and this was my reward for all my labor. Thus, I considered all my activities which my hands had done and the labor which I had exerted, and behold all was vanity and striving after wind and there was no profit under the sun.*" He had everything, yet he viewed it all as meaningless by the end of his life. I suggest you read all of Ecclesiastes chapter 2.

Solomon later said in Ecclesiastes 7:4-5, "*The mind of the wise is in the house of mourning, while the mind of fools is in the house of pleasure. It is better to listen to the rebuke of a wise man than for one to listen to the song of fools.*"

The word for *fool* used here is *kesîl*. It describes "thick-headed behavior which repeats the same mistakes over and over; foolishness; a dullard who obstinately refuses to live in reality or think seriously about life. Such is foolishly bent on self-satisfaction with lack of restraint and is out of order by doing the wrong things at the wrong times." [8]

The word for *mourning* is *ebel*, which means "to deeply grieve about something viewed as dead or seemingly fatal." [9] I am telling you these things because if you don't properly deal with any idols in your heart and rightfully turn your life to Jesus to help you overcome them, you will remain spiritually dead for eternity, separated from the presence of God. I don't want that for anyone because I know what being in God's presence means.

Here are some questions for you to ask yourself:

1. Am I willing to cut any idols or evil desires out of my life, no matter the consequences? If not, why not?
2. What am I getting from this idol that keeps me from cutting it out of my heart?
3. What am I not getting from God that keeps me using this idol to meet my needs?
4. Is there someone I can talk to about my idol to help give me clarity?

I know I have given you some difficult information and things to consider. But I want you to think back to yesterday's conversation. In Isaiah 30:18-22, I gave you the key to destroying any idols you may have in your heart. That key was a personal relationship with Jesus. The door is salvation, which is eternal life in Christ.

Tomorrow, we will discuss fasting, the tool we can use to determine if we have any areas of idolatry in our hearts. Hopefully, by now, I have given you enough information to determine what possible areas of idolatry you should start fasting from if you didn't know already.

*Before proceeding to the next section, review and ask yourself the self-reflection questions listed in the "How to Use This Devotional" section at the beginning of this book.*

# Day 3 Prayer

Father God, today I was asked a difficult question. The answer helped me realize that I have been putting something in my life before You. Father, please forgive me for not putting a relationship with You first in my life. You say in Isaiah 30 that I can destroy my idols if I set my heart to long for you, and I cry out to you, Father, for Your help. These idols are putting me on a path of destruction. I can't do this without a relationship with Jesus. Father, I need you to show me the truth about my heart. I need You to break this cycle of idolatry in my life. Father, I just need You. During this time of fasting, I want you to show me who You are and who Your Son Jesus is. Help me learn how to have a personal relationship with You. Show me Your love, so I don't need to rely on any idols to be fulfilled. Thank you for showing me the way out of my idolatry. I pray these things to You in Jesus' Mighty Name, Amen!

# Day 3 Bible Study Questions

Read John chapter 3 and answer the following questions:

1. Jesus told Nicodemus that a person had to be born again to see the Kingdom of God. What do you think that means?
    a. Why do you think Nicodemus was confused?
    b. How did Jesus respond to Nicodemus' question?
2. Why did God send Jesus into the world?
3. What is the judgment for those who do not believe in the name of the only begotten Son of God?
4. Do you remember who the light is from John chapter 1? If not, read it and think about what Jesus is saying the judgment is.
    a. What do you think John refers to when he talks about the darkness?
    b. What do we need to do before we can believe in the name of Jesus?
5. In verse 26, John's disciples (followers) were asking him why Jesus was now baptizing people. What did John say?
    a. Why did John say, "He must increase, and I must decrease?"
    b. How does this verify John's role according to chapter 1 of John?

# Day 4: What is Fasting?

Today, I will discuss the topic of fasting. I will explain:

- What fasting is
- What the Bible says about fasting
- How fasting helped me overcome my idolatry of video games
- How fasting will be used to help you determine if you are dealing with an area of idolatry in your life.

What exactly is fasting? Traditional fasting is going without food or drink for a specific period. Biblical fasting is giving up food or something else to focus your thoughts on God for a specific duration.

People with chemical addictions, such as drugs or alcohol, usually go to rehab to overcome their idols. Rehab forces them to stop using drugs in a controlled environment. This is a forced period of fasting. This allows the person to get the drugs out of their system while attempting to learn coping skills to overcome their idol.

Rehab usually isn't required for people with other types of idolatry, such as movies, television, social media, or video games. There are limited resources available to help people overcome these types of idols. Therefore, fasting can help people identify if they have made any form of entertainment an idol. Identifying the area of idolatry alone doesn't solve the problem.

In this devotional, I will use fasting to identify areas of idolatry in our lives. If we recognize an area of idolatry that keeps us from seeking Jesus, we must be willing to cut it out of our lives completely. Why do we need to be willing to cut it out?

In Mark 9:43, 45, 47, Jesus tells us why we must cut out our idols. *"If your hand causes you to stumble, cut it off; it is better for you to enter life crippled, than, having your two hands, to go into hell, into the unquenchable fire.*

*"If your foot causes you to stumble, cut it off; it is better for you to enter life lame, than, having your two feet, to be cast into hell.*

*"If your eye causes you to stumble, throw it out; it is better for you to enter the kingdom of God with one eye, than, having two eyes, to be cast into hell."*

What is Jesus saying here? He says that anything we do, anywhere we go, or anything we see that causes us to sin, cut it out. Otherwise, we are in danger of being eternally separated from God in Hell. Jesus loved us enough to warn us because He does not want that for us. He wants us to be with Him in Heaven.

Biblical fasting not only helps identify whether we have created idols in our hearts but is also the only way to remove them. We couple fasting with the cure, a relationship with Jesus. But does the Bible support a person using fasting to overcome idolatry? I believe the answer is found in Isaiah 58:6-11.

First, let me share a little context about what happened in this chapter just before these verses. The people of Israel were fasting for selfish reasons, not to seek God's will or bring themselves closer to God. They were fasting to make themselves look good and for what they thought they could get from God. That did not make God happy.

Isaiah 58:6-11 says, *"Is this not the fast which I choose, to loosen the bonds of wickedness, to undo the bands of the yoke, and to let the oppressed go free, and break every yoke? Is it not to divide your bread with the hungry, and bring the homeless poor into the house; when you see the naked, to cover him; and not to hide yourself from your own flesh?*

*"Then your light will break out like the dawn, and your recovery will speedily spring forth; and your righteousness will go before you; the glory of the Lord will be your rear guard.*

*"Then you will call, and the Lord will answer; you will cry, and He will say, 'Here I am.'*

*"If you remove the yoke from your midst, the pointing of the finger, and speaking wickedness, and if you give yourself to the hungry, and satisfy the desire of the afflicted, then your light will rise in darkness, and your gloom will become like midday.*

*"And the Lord will continually guide you, and satisfy your desire in scorched places, and give strength to your bones; And you will be like a watered garden, and like a spring of water whose waters do not fail."*

I want to go through the important parts of these verses line by line, precept by precept. Let's look at the first precept: *"to loosen the bonds of wickedness."* We first have to see how God defines wickedness. The Hebrew word for *wickedness* is *rasha*, meaning "deviating from God's standard." [1]

We must ask ourselves, "Is living in idolatry living by God's standard?" Deuteronomy 6:5 demonstrates what God's standard is for us. It says, *"You shall love the Lord your God will all your heart and with all your soul and with all your might."* I believe when we have idols in our life, we love these idols before loving God, especially if serving these idols is keeping us from seeking God completely.

What does *bonds of wickedness* mean? It means we have bound ourselves to a lifestyle outside of God's standard for us. A person who is bound can't escape or has a difficult time escaping. Fasting to escape the bonds of wickedness is what God expects. This can be applied to fasting from something we idolize.

The next precept is *"to undo the bands of the yoke."* What is a yoke? In an article on Christianity.com, Brannon Deibert defines *yoke* as "a harness used by oxen and other animals to ease the work of hauling a load. It was also meant as a designation of servitude and carrying the burden of a task or mission." [2] Another way to think of the word *yoke* is something that we are tied to that we cannot escape from on our own. An ox had to wait for his owner to remove the yoke. We need Jesus to help us remove our idols. In this precept, God says that fasting can help us seek Him so He can remove the things in life that have us tied down. This can be applied to idolatry as well.

The next precept is *"and let the oppressed go free."* I can't speak for anyone other than myself, but I was oppressed by my video game idolatry. While playing video games, I felt trapped, not wanting to stop playing, even though a part of me knew I was hurting those around me. I didn't know how to be set free from it. The Hebrew word for *oppressed* is *rāṣaṣ*. It means "to render incapable, so something no longer functions in its natural or rightful capacity." [3] I was not functioning the way God said I should when playing my video games. This precept says fasting will set us free from what oppresses us.

I will skip down to the last precept in Isaiah 58:7, *"and not hide yourself from your own flesh."* The Hebrew word for *hide* is *'ālam*. It means "what is hidden, unknowable unless revealed." [4] The Hebrew word for *flesh* is *basar*. It can mean lustful desires of the flesh. It is saying not to hide from yourself the knowledge of your own lustful desires. Our lustful desires refer to our sinful ways. Fasting while seeking Jesus can lead us to accept the truth of our sinful ways. Once we can acknowledge our sin, we can submit it to Jesus. His blood washes away our sin when we acknowledge our sin to Him in agreement with Him.

The word *then* in Hebrew is *āz* which means "at that time." As we are fasting, God is helping us remove our wickedness, breaking our yoke of bondage, and removing from us what is oppressing us. Then (at that time), the following things will occur. Isaiah 58:8-11 tells us how God uses our fasting so that He can continually guide us, satisfy our desires, give us strength, and continually fill us with living water.

Verse 8 says, *"Then your light will break out like the dawn, and your recovery will speedily spring forth."* God says fasting while seeking Him leads to our recovery. When we stop worshipping our idols and seek Jesus, we will have a breakthrough. We seek Jesus by reading the Bible, going to church, and letting someone who knows God disciple us. This will lead us to a speedy recovery from our idolatry. It also leads us to a personal relationship with Jesus. I experienced this firsthand. I want to share that with you.

In 2018, my church had a church-wide period of Biblical fasting. Most of the time, that means fasting from food. But my pastor explained fasting from a different perspective. He said that we could choose to fast from anything that keeps us from seeking a relationship with Jesus.

During this time, I was having marital problems. One of the significant factors causing problems in my marriage was my excessive video game usage. At the time, I didn't identify myself as having an idol. But I knew that playing video games was not only causing problems in my marriage but keeping me from seeking a closer, more personal relationship with Jesus. So, I chose to fast from video games during this church-wide fasting period.

As I got to personally know Jesus by reading the Bible, I felt something like a fire light inside me. I started feeling happier, less depressed, and more spiritually alive than I had ever felt. During this time of fasting, I also had the strength to do things I had never done before. I dieted for the first time in my life. While doing so, I lost 30 pounds. I also realized that I knew about Jesus but had never met Jesus in a personal way. This encounter with Jesus started changing me from the inside.

While fasting and seeking Jesus by reading the Bible, my desire to play video games was gone. I really enjoyed learning about Jesus. I actually spent three months fasting from my video games and seeking Jesus. I read the whole New Testament and a book on the study of Revelation. As I said previously in my testimony, I didn't completely destroy my idol then, but my encounter with Jesus led me to destroy my idol a couple of months later. I genuinely believe that had I not done this Biblical fast, I would have never destroyed my idol.

When you read yesterday about different things you could have as idols, did you identify any areas of your life that you could be putting before Jesus, causing you physical, psychological, or social harm? If not, that is a great thing. Maybe you identified some bad habits that need to be addressed. I challenge you to pick one, only one, of those possible idols or bad habits you want to overcome and commit to fasting from that while you are reading this daily devotional.

If you are dealing with substance abuse, I would advise you to seek guidance from a physician or a local rehabilitation program to support you during this time of fasting. I don't want you to fast from something alone without the proper medical guidance. The last thing I want is for anyone to suffer harshly from withdrawal symptoms without the proper medical assistance to help them through it. You can still use this devotional to draw you to a closer relationship with Jesus while under a physician's care or rehab.

If you have set up an idol in your heart, you will feel loss, anger, resentment, frustration, or sadness. You may feel a strong urge to return to your idol for the first few days at least. If you feel that urge, reach out to someone who loves you or the person you are doing this devotional with for help.

During your fast, if you have no problems taking time away from the possible area of idolatry and are not feeling those symptoms listed above at any time, it may not be an idol for you. You could just have a bad habit that you need to correct. If you don't think you are having a problem in that area after a few days of fasting and you have another possible idol in mind, it's okay to change the one you are fasting from. Just keep doing the devotional and moving forward. Do that until you either run out of possible areas of idolatry, or you find an area of idolatry or a bad habit you want to address.

You must read the Bible each day, seek Jesus, pray to Jesus for help, and be totally honest with yourself. If you are doing these things, you will see a change in your life, no matter whether you idolize something.

If you do identify an idol in your life, talk to Jesus. Tell Jesus that you don't want to keep loving this idol more than Him. Ask Him to help you remove this idol from your life and believe that He will. Keep seeking Jesus daily, even after you finish this book.

Review the self-reflection questions to journal again today. While fasting, truthfully answer these questions daily to help you self-reflect on how you feel about the possible area of idolatry you are fasting from. Write down your answers and compare them daily to see if there is a change in how you feel during this process. Look for both positive and negative changes.

In the next chapter, we are going to learn about God. Who is He? Why did He create us? What does He expect from us? What is His purpose for us today?

> *Before proceeding to the next section, review and ask yourself the self-reflection questions listed in the "How to Use This Devotional" section at the beginning of this book.*

# Day 4 Prayer

Father God, today, I learned more about fasting. I learned that You want me to fast because it draws me closer to You, Father. I want to become closer to You and Your Son, Jesus. I have been searching my heart, Father, and I realized some areas of my life have not been by Your standard. These areas are _____. Father, as I am fasting from these things in my life, I fully submit these areas to You. I need Your help. I know I can't do this alone. I pray to You, Father, that You loosen the bonds of wickedness that is the idol in my heart, undo the bands of the yoke of idolatry that is keeping me from You, help me destroy this idol that is oppressing me, and open my eyes to reveal to me the lustful desires of my heart so I can submit them to You. You say, Father, that if I fast and set my heart to long for You, Father, my recovery will quickly spring forth. I believe you, Father! I pray that You give me Your strength to face my idol and destroy it by the blood of Your Son, Jesus, who died for me so I could be set free. I believe You, God, and thank You for loving me enough to not give up on me. I love You, God, and ask You to hear my prayers and answer them. In Jesus Mighty Name, I pray, amen.

# Day 4 Bible Study Questions

Read John chapter 4 and answer the following questions:

1.  When Jesus was speaking to the woman at the well, what do you think was the living water Jesus was referring to?
    a.  What kind of thirst do you think Jesus is talking about?
2.  How do you think Jesus knew she was telling him a lie about having no husband?
3.  Who did the woman say He was?
4.  When Jesus revealed Himself as the Messiah to the woman, what did she do?
    a.  What did she say to the people about Jesus?
    b.  What was the result of her actions later on?
5.  What kind of food did Jesus say He had?
6.  Why did Jesus heal the royal official's son?
    a.  Because he believed and his son was healed, what did it say about his household when he told them what had happened?
    b.  What does that say about the power of your testimony?

# Day 5: Who is God?

Today we are going to talk about God. As a disclaimer, I want to say no one can truly understand the wholeness of God. I could write 1,000 pages of a book about God and barely scratch the surface. That being said, I will limit the scope of this discussion to a general understanding of God. I will discuss a few of the Bible's descriptions of God. I will then discuss His purpose for creating us, a little of what He expects from us, and finally, His purpose for us today.

The first way God is introduced in the Bible is as Creator. Genesis chapters 1 and 2 describe how God created the heavens and earth and everything in it out of nothing. As He was creating everything, He called it all good. God created space, which is the heavens and the Earth [1] and time, which was when He created the light, separated it from the darkness, calling the light day and the darkness night and defined the amount of time in a day. [2] Since God existed before He created space and time, He is not subject to either one; He exists outside of space and time. As you keep reading Genesis chapter 1, you will see how God created everything—the oceans, land, sky, stars, planets, vegetation, plants, and all the living creatures in land, in the waters, and in the air—and He called it all good. [3] He did all this in only five days. God created everything to bring glory to Himself.

Next, Genesis 1:26-27 (AMP) says, *"Then God said, 'Let Us (Father, Son, Holy Spirit) make man in Our image, according to Our likeness [not physical, but a spiritual personality and moral likeness]; and let them have complete authority over the fish of the sea, the birds of the air, and over everything that creeps and crawls on the earth.' So, God created man in His own image, in the image and likeness of God He created him; male and female He created them."* God created everything else first, then He created mankind. But He created us different because we were created in His image. That sets us apart from everything else in God's creation. The purpose for which He created us is to aid Him in caring for everything He created. Isn't that amazing that God cared enough about us to give us a special purpose?

Genesis chapter 2 gives a more detailed explanation of how He created mankind. But at the end of Genesis chapter 1, verse 31 says, *"God saw everything He had made, and behold, it was very good."* God made everything perfect. He couldn't have made it any better. But something happened that changed that; sin entered the world. We are going to talk more about that in tomorrow's discussion.

God is Holy. Psalm 99:1-5 says, *"The Lord reigns, let the peoples tremble; He is enthroned above the cherubim, let the earth shake! The Lord is great in Zion, and He is exalted above all the peoples. Let them praise Your great and awesome name; Holy is He. The strength of the King loves justice; You have established justice and righteousness in Jacob. Exalt the Lord our God and worship at His footstool; Holy is He."* The Hebrew word for *holy* is *qadosh* which means "what stands apart." [4] God created everything with order for His own pleasure. God will not allow Himself to be in the presence of sin, which is disobedience to His order in which He created everything.

God is a just God. He is honest and always keeps His word. Psalms 33:4-5 says, *"For the word of the Lord is upright; and all His work is done in faithfulness. He loves righteousness and justice; The earth is full of the lovingkindness of the Lord."* Psalms 111:7-8 says, *"The works of His hands are truth and justice; All His precepts are sure. They are upheld forever and ever; They are performed in truth and uprightness."* The Word of God is trustworthy. He can't lie because He created the truth and is the truth Himself.

God created us for a purpose, to love Him and love one another. Deuteronomy 6:5 says, *"You shall love the Lord your God with all your heart and with all your soul and with all your might."* God's original purpose for us was to be in relationship with Him. Because He loves us and desires for us to love Him, He is patient and gracious to us to give us time to realize we need to be reconciled to Him. [5]

God expects us to desire to be in relationship with Him and to submit ourselves to His will for us. He expects this because He knows better than we how we should live our lives because He created us.

Isaiah 55:6-9 says, *"Seek the Lord while He may be found; Call upon Him while He is near. Let the wicked forsake his way and the unrighteous man his thoughts; and let him return to the Lord, and He will have compassion on him, and to our God, for He will abundantly pardon. 'For my thoughts are not your thoughts, nor are your ways my ways,' declares the Lord. 'For as the heavens are higher than the earth, so are My ways higher than your ways and My thoughts than your thoughts.'"*

God wants us to obey Him because He wants things to go well for us. He loves us and desires that relationship He created us to have with Him to be restored. But He won't force us to obey; it has to voluntarily come from us because that's how we show God that we love him.

God's purpose for us now is to be His ambassadors. God is establishing His Kingdom on earth and wants us to be a part of it. The Greek word for *ambassador* is *presbeuō*, which means we are "to be representatives of God's kingdom properly communicating the policies of the kingdom of heaven with accuracy and credibility." [6] 2 Corinthians 5:20 says, *"Therefore, we are ambassadors for Christ, as though*

*God were making an appeal through us; we beg you on behalf of Christ, be reconciled to God."* We are to go out into the world after we are saved and share the good news of Jesus with all people everywhere.

Finally, Jesus' command for us is the great commission found in Matthew 28:18-20. It reads, *"And Jesus came up and spoke to them, saying, "All authority has been given to me in heaven and on earth. Go therefore and make disciples of all the nations, baptizing them in the name of the Father and the Son and the Holy Spirit, teaching them to observe all that I commanded you; and lo, I am with you always, even to the end of the age."*

This book aims to help you recognize any idols in your life so that you can remove them. These idols are keeping you separated from a relationship with God. I want you to be reconciled to Him through His Son Jesus so that you, too, can do the good works God has prepared in advance for you to do.

> *Before proceeding to the next section, review and ask yourself the self-reflection questions listed in the "How to Use This Devotional" section at the beginning of this book.*

# Day 5 Prayer

Father God, today I learned about who You are. You are the Creator of all things in heaven and on earth. You created them to bring You glory, God. I thank You for that, Father. But You also created me in Your own Image, so I could have a relationship with You. But Father, I have not been seeking you in my life, and I want that to change. Please, Father, show me the way to be reconciled to You. Help me learn how to show You love the way You want me to. Help me, Father, to learn how to be a part of Your Kingdom, fulfilling Your purpose for me to be Your Ambassador for Christ. Help me learn how to go out and make disciples of all people. As I seek you, Father, reveal Yourself to me more and more every day so I can know You in every way that I possibly can. I thank You again, Father, for loving me, showing me mercy and compassion, and giving me time to realize that I need You in my life. I ask you, Father, for all these things in Jesus' Mighty Name, Amen.

# Day 5 Bible Study Questions

Read John chapter 5 and answer the following questions:

1. What was the first thing Jesus said to the man lying at the pool at Bethesda?
    a. Why do you think Jesus asked this question?
    b. How did the man respond?
2. Do you think the man was making an excuse for himself why he was still in that condition, or do you think he was truly doing his best to help himself?
    a. Why?
3. What did Jesus tell him to do after the man gave his answer?
    a. Why did the man not question Jesus when he told him what to do?
4. Why were the Jews questioning the man about being healed?
    a. What day was it that this event occurred?
5. The man who was healed didn't know who had healed him. Why do you think this information was necessary for John to include?
6. What did Jesus tell the man he healed at the temple?
    a. Why did Jesus tell him this?
    b. What does this show us that Jesus expects for those he has healed?
7. What were two reasons why the Jews wanted to kill Jesus?
8. What did Jesus say to them about his Father?
    a. What do you think this means?
9. What were the 4 different ways that Jesus had to testify of Him?

# Day 6: What is Sin?

Today we are going to spend some time talking about sin. First, we will explain what sin is, followed by some examples of sin. Second, we will discuss what happened that caused sin to enter the world. Third, we will discuss the consequences of sin. Last but certainly not least, we will briefly discuss how God made a way to overcome our sin.

Yesterday, we discussed how God created everything, called it good, and gave it order and purpose, even mankind. [1] Sin, simply put, is anything done that falls outside of God's order of creation. That includes doing something in the way God never designed for us to do. Or not doing something in the way God said we should.

Let's look at an example. Genesis 1:27 says, *"So God created man in His image, in the image of God He created him; male and female He created them."* God created me as a biological male. This truth is something that is final and can never be truly changed. If I act as a female, that falls outside God's design for me. This is sin for me. Why? Because by doing this, I am saying that I know better about who I am than God, who created me this way. Simply put, I know better than God. That is putting myself in the place of God.

This is called self-idolatry. God created us to worship Him, fellowship with Him, and love Him in divine reverence. How do I know this? Look at the first two of the ten commandments God gave to Moses, also known as the Law of Moses. Exodus 20:3-5 says, *"You shall have no other gods before Me. You shall not make for yourself any idol, or any likeness of what is in heaven above or on the earth beneath or in the water under the earth. You shall not worship them nor serve them; for I, the Lord your God, am a jealous God."*

I will list the basic description of the ten commandments [2] given to Moses by God. These commandments are supposed to help reveal to us that *"we all have sinned and fallen short of the glory of God."* [3] They are as follows:

1. *You shall have no other gods before me.*
2. *You shall not make for yourself any idol...or worship them or serve them.*
3. *You shall not take the name of the Lord your God in vain.*
4. *Remember the Sabbath day to keep it holy.*
5. *Honor your father and your mother.*
6. *You shall not commit murder.*
7. *You shall not commit adultery.*
8. *You shall not steal.*
9. *You shall not testify falsely against your neighbor.*
10. *You shall not covet...anything that belongs to your neighbor.*

These are the laws God gave to Moses for the nation of Israel. He expected them to follow these laws. God created these laws to give order to the people because they were hurting each other. This is part of God's order for us as well. God loves all of His creation. He doesn't want us to hurt each other.

Now let's discuss how sin entered the world in the first place. This event is described in Genesis chapter 3. Let's first discuss the order that God created for mankind in the beginning. He created man and called him Adam. The first thing God did after He made Adam is found in Genesis 2:15-17. *"So the Lord God took the man and settled him in the Garden of Eden to cultivate and keep it. And the Lord God commanded the man saying, 'You may freely eat from every tree of the garden; but from the tree of the knowledge of good and evil you shall not eat, otherwise on the day that you eat from it, you shall most certainly die.'"* The first rules God gave Adam were to tend to the Garden of Eden and not eat the fruit of the tree of knowledge of good and evil. And He told Adam the consequences if he disobeyed.

What were the consequences? God told Adam that disobedience would lead to death. Let's look forward to what the Apostle Paul said about sin. In Romans 6:23, Paul said, *"For the wages of sin is death..."* Sin is a challenging topic for us to discuss because it goes against our carnal nature.

Next, God shows us that He not only wants us to be in relationship with Him, but He wants us to be in relationship with one another. Genesis 2:18 says, *"Now the Lord God said, 'It is not good for the man to be alone; I will make him a helper suitable for him.'"* God then goes on to explain how He created woman out of the rib of Adam. [4]

Genesis 2:24 is the first command God gave Adam and the woman (Eve). *"For this reason a man shall leave his father and his mother and shall be joined to his wife; and they shall become one flesh."* He commanded them to marry and become husband and wife, thus creating the first institution, the family.

The next commandment God gave them is recorded in Genesis 1:28: *"And God blessed them and said to them, 'Be fruitful, multiply, and fill the earth, and subjugate it; and rule over the fish of the sea, the birds of the air, and every living thing that moves upon the earth.'"* God told them to reproduce and gave them dominion over the earth to rule alongside creation with Him.

Let's look at what happens next in Genesis 3:1-13:

> *Now the serpent was more crafty than any beast*
> *of the field which the Lord God had made. And he said*

*to the woman, "Indeed, has God said, 'You shall not eat from any tree of the garden'?" The woman said to the serpent, "From the fruit of the trees of the garden we may eat; but from the fruit of the tree which is in the middle of the garden, God has said, 'You shall not eat from it or touch it, or you will die.'" The serpent said to the woman, "You surely will not die! For God knows that in the day you eat from it your eyes will be opened, and you will be like God, knowing good and evil." When the woman saw that the tree was good for food, and that it was a delight to the eyes, and that the tree was desirable to make one wise, she took from its fruit and ate; and she gave also to her husband with her, and he ate. Then the eyes of both of them were opened, and they knew that they were naked; and they sewed fig leaves together and made themselves loin coverings.*

*They heard the sound of the Lord God walking in the garden in the cool of the day, and the man and his wife hid themselves from the presence of the Lord God among the trees of the garden. Then the Lord God called to the man, and said to him, "Where are you?" He said, "I heard the sound of You in the garden, and I was afraid because I was naked; so I hid myself." And He said, "Who told you that you were naked? Have you eaten from the tree of which I commanded you not to eat?" The man said, "The woman whom You gave to be with me, she gave me from the tree, and I ate." Then the Lord God said to the woman, "What is this you have done?" And the woman said, "The serpent deceived me, and I ate."*

The serpent, Satan, came and tempted the woman, Eve, by asking her, "Did God really say?" He included some truth with the lies. Adam and Eve disobeyed God's commandment. What were the results of their disobedience? They first became aware of their sin, which we call shame. Once aware of their sin, they hid from God, realizing they were naked and had messed up. God gave them a chance to tell the truth about their actions. The woman blamed the serpent, and Adam blamed both God and the woman. The other physical consequences are described in Genesis 3:14-19. Read about them when you get a chance. But what about the death that God said would happen?

Genesis 3:22-24 says, *"Then the Lord God said, 'Behold, the man has become like one of Us, knowing good and evil; and now, lest he stretch out his hand, and take also from the tree of life, and eat, and live forever' — therefore the Lord God sent him out from the garden of Eden, to cultivate the ground from which he was taken. So, He drove the man out; and at the east of the garden of Eden He stationed the cherubim, and the flaming sword which turned every direction, to guard the way to the tree of life."*

The death God was telling them would come was actually spiritual death. This is separation from the presence of God. Because they disobeyed God and sinned, God had to cast them out to protect them. God knew that they had knowledge of evil in their hearts now and were corrupted. If He allowed them to stay in the garden, they could eat from the tree of life and be stuck in their sinful condition forever. So, He cast them out of His presence because He loved them. He wanted them to have a chance to be reconciled to Him.

The consequence of our sin is we become separated from the presence of God. Jesus said during His sermon on the mount in Matthew 5:18-19, *"For I assure you and most solemnly say to you, until heaven and earth pass away, not the smallest letter or stroke will pass from the Law until all things are accomplished. So, whoever breaks one of the least of the commandments, and teaches others to do the same, will be called least in the king-dom of heaven; but whoever practices and teaches them, he will be called great in the kingdom of heaven."*

Have you ever lied, stolen something, gossiped about someone, or lived life the way you thought was best for you instead of what God says is best for you? If you have done only one of these things, you have *"sinned and fallen short of the glory of God."* [3] If you choose to remain in this sinful state, you can never be in the presence of God. If you die this way, you will be eternally separated from God in hell. I am not telling you this to condemn you to hell. Let me explain.

We learned yesterday that God loves us. He is a just God. Because He is a just God, He wants us to have a chance to be forgiven and restored to relationship with Him. But we cannot do that on our own. We need help. We will discuss where this help comes from tomorrow, but I do not want to leave you discouraged. Now, let us see what the second part of Romans 6:23 says: *"For the wages of sin is death, but the free gift of God is eternal life in Christ Jesus our Lord."* God loves us so much He made a way for us to be reconciled to Him. The way is through His Son Jesus. Tomorrow, we will answer the question, "Who is Jesus?"

The purpose of this book is to help reveal the sin of idolatry, which is how God sees addiction, so that you can stop doing it. For the remainder of this book, we will discuss how to overcome our idolatry by seeking a relationship with Jesus.

Jesus says in John 3:19-20, *"This is the judgment, that the Light has come into the world, and men loved the darkness rather than the Light, for their deeds were evil. For everyone who does evil hates the Light, and does not come to the Light for fear that his deeds will be exposed."* Jesus is referring to Himself as being the Light. He says, *"men loved the darkness rather than the Light."*

The word for *darkness* used here is *skotos*. Figuratively, *skotos* means "the principle of sin carrying its certain results." [5] Jesus is saying that people loved their sinful ways more than Him. From this context, we could easily say that Jesus calls all sin an idol. While we will be focusing on overcoming our idols, any sin we commit is an idol since it keeps us from God. When I say in the rest of the book to turn from any idols, other sins listed in the Bible are included by default. We must turn away from our sin and seek a personal relationship with Jesus.

*Before proceeding to the next section, review and ask yourself the self-reflection questions listed in the "How to Use This Devotional" section at the beginning of this book.*

*Additional questions to ask yourself during fasting for self-reflection:*

1. *What did you learn today about sin?*
2. *Did you recognize any areas of life that you have unrepented sin?*
3. *How does it feel to know that even though you have sinned God still loves you and made a way for you to be forgiven?*

# Day 6 Prayer

Father God, today I learned what sin is. Sin is what keeps me separated from You. Search my heart, O Father God, and reveal any active areas of sin in my life. When you do, Father, help me to have the desire to stop sinning and to submit myself as holy and pleasing to you. "Save me, O God, for the waters have threatened my life. I have sunk in deep mire, where there is no foothold; I have come into deep waters, where a flood overwhelms me. I am weary with my crying; my throat is parched; my eyes fail while I wait for my God. O God, You know my folly; my wrongs are not hidden from You. When I wept and humbled myself with fasting, it became my reproach. But as for me, my prayer is to You, O Lord, at an acceptable and opportune time; O God, in the greatness of Your favor and in the abundance of Your lovingkindness, answer me with truth. Rescue me from the mire and do not let me sink; let me be rescued from those who hate me and from the deep waters. Do not let the floodwater overwhelm me, nor the deep waters swallow me up, nor the pit shut its mouth over me. Answer me, O Lord, for Your lovingkindness is sweet and good and comforting; according to the greatness of Your compassion, turn to me. Do not hide Your face from Your servant, for I am in distress; answer me quickly. Draw near to my soul and redeem it; ransom me because of my enemies." [6] I pray these things to you in Jesus' mighty name, Amen!

# Day 6 Bible Study Questions

Read John chapter 6 and answer the following questions:

1. Jesus asked Phillip where they could go buy some food for the crowd of people there with Jesus.
    a. Why did Jesus ask Phillip this?
2. What did Jesus do for the people with five loaves of bread and two fish?
    a. From what we have learned about Jesus so far, why was Jesus able to do this?
3. How many baskets were they able to fill with the leftover crumbs of bread?
4. What did the people say about Jesus when they saw Him perform this miracle?
5. During the storm, why were the disciples frightened when they saw Jesus?
    a. What did they think He was?
6. Why did Jesus say that the people were seeking Jesus?
    a. What did Jesus tell them they should be working for?
    b. Where does this food come from?
7. The people asked Jesus, "What then do You do for a sign, so that we may see, and believe you? What work do You perform? Our fathers ate the manna in the wilderness; as it is written, 'HE GAVE THEM BREAD OUT OF HEAVEN TO EAT.'" Who did Jesus say that the bread came from?
    a. What did the bread do?
    b. Who was Jesus really referring to as bread?
    c. What happens to those who eat the bread

that comes out of Heaven?

8. What did Jesus say that gives us life?

    a. What did Jesus say to his disciples are spirit and life?

# Day 7: Who is Jesus?

We have already learned a lot about Jesus so far. Let's take a minute to review what we know. Jesus is a real man who loves you. He wants to have a personal relationship with you. He died for you so you could be saved.

Jesus is *"the way, the truth and the life the only way to the Father."* [1] Jesus was the Word, and He was with God in the beginning. [2] He is the light. [3] He is *"the Lamb of God that takes the sin away from the world."* [4] He is *"the Son of God."* [5] He is a teacher. [6] He performs miracles. [7]

He has *"been given all Authority on heaven and on earth."* [8] He is the way for eternal life and salvation. [9] He is the source of the living water. [10] He is a prophet. [11] He is the Messiah. [12] He is a healer. [13]

Think about this, if the Bible says that Jesus is all of these things, don't you think it could be worth something for you to take some time to get to know Him more personally? Our goal for today is to learn about some of these descriptions of Jesus in a deeper way.

Like I said in my testimony, it's best to start learning about Jesus from the beginning. Jesus was with God in the beginning. How? Because Jesus Himself is the Son of God, a part of the Godhead, the triune nature of God. Let's look again at John 1:1-3: *"In the beginning was the Word, and the Word was with God, and the Word was God. He was in the beginning with God. All things came into being through Him, and apart from Him nothing came into being that has come into being."*

John describes Jesus as two things, the Word of God and God Himself. To understand this concept, we must understand God's triune nature. With our limited human understanding, this is one of the most difficult concepts to understand, so just bear with me.

The word that describes God is *theós,* which means "God, the creator and owner of all things. Theós refers to the God of the Bible, who is eternally existent in three Persons, in one undivided (infinitely personal) Essence. The three persons are God, the Father; God the Son (Jesus); and God, the Holy Spirit." [14] They are all part of the same Essence, but each plays a distinct role according to the Bible.

Genesis 1:1-3 says, *"In the beginning God created the heavens and the earth. And the earth was formless and void, and darkness was over the surface of the deep; and the Spirit of God was moving over the surface of the waters. Then God said, 'Let there be light'; and there was light."*

God was present, the Spirit of God was present, and God said, which means He spoke Words. I believe—and this is my own personal understanding—that when God speaks, Jesus is the one who carries out His request. Jesus said in John 5:30: *"I can do nothing on My own initiative. As I hear, I judge, and My judgement is just, because I do not seek My own will, but the will of Him who sent Me."* And later in John 5:36: *"But the testimony which I have is greater than the testimony of John; for the works which the Father has given me to accomplish — the very works that I do — testify about Me, that the father has sent Me."* These verses, along with John 1:1, are the reason I believe Jesus carries out what the Father says to do.

Now that we understand that God and Jesus are part of the same Essence, let's move on to the next title Jesus is called, Immanuel. Matthew 1:18-25 describes the birth of Jesus. Let's look closer at Matthew 1:23: *"Behold, the virgin shall be with child and shall bear a son, and they shall call His name, Immanuel," which translated means, "God with us."* An angel was speaking this to Joseph, Jesus' earthly father, the husband of Mary, Jesus' mother. This verse was an Old Testament prophecy [15,] which the angel told Joseph their son would fulfill.

Let's review before moving forward. Jesus is the Son of God, who is God, is the Word of God and was with God in the beginning during creation. Through Jesus, all things came into being. Jesus was born of a virgin, Mary, through the Holy Spirit that came into Mary, conceiving Jesus. And Jesus, being all God and all man, was born into the world and given the title by an angel, Immanuel, which means "God with us."

The next title that was given to Jesus was "the Messiah." Matthew 1:18 says, *"Jacob was the father of Joseph, the husband of Mary, by whom Jesus was born, who is called the Messiah."* Messiah is the Hebrew word, but the word in Greek is *Xristós*, the Christ, which literally means "the anointed one. Jesus, the Christ accomplished His full objective by His earthly ministry—and did so by the uninterrupted power (anointing) of the Holy Spirit. Jesus was always and exactly directed by God, through the anointing (teaching) of the Holy Spirit—performing all the Father's will" [16].

Jesus was sent to earth for a purpose by God, the Father. The purpose is described in Hebrews 12:2. *"...fixing our eyes on Jesus, the author and perfecter of faith, who for the joy set before Him endured the cross, despising the shame, and has sat down at the right hand of the throne of God."* He came to be the author and perfecter of faith. He sacrificed Himself on the cross so that we have the opportunity to be reconciled to God [17]. Three days after Jesus died, He was resurrected by God. In His resurrected form, Jesus revealed Himself to his disciples and five hundred witnesses. [18] He then rose to Heaven to be seated at the right hand of God. [19]

The last title we will discuss today is "Advocate."

In 1 John 2:1-2, John says, *"My little children, I am writing these things to you so that you may not sin. And if anyone sins, we have an Advocate with the Father, Jesus Christ the righteous; and He Himself is the propitiation for our sins; and not for ours only, but also for those of the whole world."* John is saying that Jesus paid the cost not only for our sins but for everyone who believes in Him. Now that we know more about Jesus, tomorrow, we will discuss why we need Him.

*Before proceeding to the next section, review and ask yourself the self-reflection questions listed in the "How to Use This Devotional" section at the beginning of this book.*

# Day 7 Prayer

Father God, I learned a lot today about Your Son Jesus. I learned that Jesus loves me. I learned that You sent Jesus to be born on the earth through the virgin Mary so that I have a chance to be reconciled to You. I learned that Jesus was with You from the beginning and all things created were created through Him. I learned that Jesus lived a perfect life on earth. I learned that Jesus was the Author and Perfecter of faith, that He sacrificed Himself by dying on a cross so that I can be saved from eternal separation from You, Father, because I am a sinner. Thank you, Father, for not giving up on me and the rest of the world. Thank you for coming down to earth and experiencing what I experience so that You can show grace and mercy to me by allowing Jesus to be my Advocate at Your Right Hand. Father, please help me to see where I stand in my relationship with You. Open up my eyes to reveal any sinful ways that I may have. If you reveal to me any sin, Father, give me the courage to admit that sin to myself and to You. I ask this in Your Son, Jesus' Mighty Name. Amen.

# Day 7 Bible Study Questions

Read John chapter 7 and answer the following questions:

1.  Why did Jesus tell His brothers that the world hates Him?
2.  At the feast of booths in Judea, what were the crowds arguing about?
3.  When the Jews heard Jesus teaching at the temple, they were surprised that Jesus could teach like that, having not been formally taught.
    a.  How did Jesus respond to them?
4.  Who did Jesus say His teaching came from?
5.  What point was Jesus making about His accusers in His response to their claim that He had a demon?
6.  When Jesus says, "You will seek Me, and will not find Me; and where I am, you cannot come." Where do you think Jesus will be going?
7.  What does it say that Jesus is speaking of when He says, "He who believes in Me, as the Scripture said, 'From his innermost being will flow rivers of living water.'"?
8.  Why do you think Nicodemus spoke up in defense of Jesus, saying He should have a chance to testify for Himself?

# Day 8: Why Do I Need Jesus?

The question for discussion today is, "Why do I need Jesus?" Before we answer this question, I want us to review what we have learned. In the first two days, we learned that addiction is a substance, activity, or behavior we repeatedly do over a long period of time that causes us, or those around us, physical, psychological, or social harm as well as negative feelings such as anxiety, irritability, tremors, or nausea. We also discussed how addiction, if it keeps us from seeking a relationship with Jesus, is an idol to us. We also learned that idolatry is a sin against God.

On day four, we learned about fasting and how it can be used Biblically as a tool for helping us to be healed from our addiction. We also learned that to be healed with fasting, we must start seeking a personal relationship with Jesus. We can do this by reading about Jesus in the Bible, going to church, praying to God, asking for His help, and helping each other grow in the faith through discipleship.

On day five, we learned a little about God. We learned that He created everything out of nothing, gave it order, and called it good. He then uniquely created us in His Image and Likeness so that He could have a personal relationship with us and rule over His creation with Him. But Adam and Eve were deceived into disobeying God by eating the fruit from the tree of knowledge of good and evil. This broke God's heart because He is good and cannot be in the presence of evil. God cast them out of the Garden of Eden because they sinned against Him and to give mankind an opportunity to be restored to a relationship with God.

On day six, we learned about sin. Sin is anything we do that falls outside of the order God created us to live by and separates us from God. God gave Moses the Law to help us realize that we have sinned against Him. God wants us to turn away from our sin and return to following His order of creation. God made a plan for us to restore our relationship with Him. That plan involved His son Jesus.

Finally, on day seven, we learned about Jesus and that He was not only the Son of God but a part of the essence of God Himself. God made everything that was made through Jesus. God had a plan to use Jesus from the beginning to die for us on the cross so that He could pay the cost of our sins. Jesus loved us so much that He sacrificed Himself for us because it pleased His Father to do so.

All of these truths must be brought together to answer the question, "Why do I need Jesus?" God loves us, but our relationship with God has been broken because Adam sinned. God wanted to restore that relationship, so He gave Moses the Law to help people recognize their sins and need for God. But the law was never meant to save anyone. Jesus, the Christ, is the only one who can save us from our sinful state.

How did He do that? He came to earth as God with us to put on human flesh and experience what we experience. He came to live life in perfect obedience to the will of His Father, God. That way, He could offer Himself up as an acceptable blood sacrifice to pay the cost of our sins on the cross so that we could be reconciled to God.

What happens if someone chooses not to believe in Jesus? Remember, I said that God exists outside of space and time? God already knows that some people will refuse to believe in Jesus and be reconciled to Him. Look at what Jesus said in John 3:16-21:

*"For God so loved the world, that He gave His only begotten Son, that whoever believes in Him shall not perish, but have eternal life. For God did not send the Son into the world to judge the world, but that the world might be saved through Him. He who believes in Him is not judged; he who does not believe has been judged already, because he has not believed in the name of the only begotten Son of God.*

*"This is the judgment, that the Light has come into the world, and men loved the darkness rather than the Light, for their deeds were evil. For everyone who does evil hates the Light, and does not come to the Light for fear that his deeds will be exposed. But he who practices the truth comes to the Light, so that his deeds may be manifested as having been wrought in God."*

For me, these verses are bittersweet. We get to see God's love for us as well as the way we can be saved through Jesus. That's good news. But Jesus tells the truth next. He says those who do not believe in Him have already been judged. What is the judgment? Men love the darkness rather than the Light and do not come to the Light for fear that their deeds will be exposed. Simply put, men choose Hell over Heaven because of their love of sin, which is idolatry.

The word for *darkness* in this verse is *skótos*. This word means "the principle of sin carrying its certain results." Darkness also refers to "the realm in which God's light is obscured to people who prefer sin." [1] In other words, a person will never leave the darkness and will experience eternal death outside the presence of God until that person hears the law, chooses to recognize their sin for what it is, and turns their life to Jesus.

What does the Bible say this death will be like? Matthew 13:41-42 says, *"The Son of Man will send forth His angels, and they will gather out of His kingdom all stumbling blocks, and those who commit lawlessness, and will throw them into the furnace of fire; in that place there will be weeping and gnashing of teeth."* This is a description of Hell. For more examples, see the following verses: Matthew 13:49-50; Matthew 22:13; Matthew 24:50-51.

The furnace of fire is talking about Hell. The word used for Hell was *Gehenna, "which was also re*ferred to as "the lake of fire" in *Revelation.* Gehenna is the place of post-resurrection torment (judgment) and strictly refers to the everlasting abode of the unredeemed. Here they experience divine judgment in their individual resurrection-bodies given to them at the Great White Throne Judgment [2]. Each unredeemed person receives a body which bears their (unique) judgment, i.e., has the capacity to "match" their torment (commensurate with their divine judgment)." [3]

Matthew 10:28 says, *"Do not fear those who kill the body but are unable to kill the soul; but rather fear Him who is able to destroy both soul and body in hell."* What point do you think Jesus is making with this statement?

I believe He is saying that we should be more afraid of the eternal spiritual death leading to Hell than the physical death of the body. The rightful fear of eternal separation from God should lead us to repentance and eternal life with Jesus. Then our physical death is just an event bound to happen but not to be feared.

I want to discuss what the phrase "weeping and gnashing of teeth" means. The word for *weeping* is *klauthmós.* It means "bitter grief that springs from feeling utterly hopeless. It is usually accompanied by shrieks brought on by uncontainable emotional pain." [4] The word used for *teeth, odoús,* "metaphorically describes the unredeemed in Gehenna expressing their indescribable agony by 'the gnashing of teeth'" [5] These feelings of utter hopelessness and agony will be felt for eternity in Hell.

The lake of fire was meant for Satan and his demons, the fallen angels, that rebelled with him against God. [6] Revelation 20:10 says, *"And the devil who deceived them was thrown into the lake of fire and brimstone, where the beast and the false prophet are also; and they will be tormented day and night forever and ever."* The people in hell with the devil and his demons will be tormented day and night for eternity. Revelation 21:8 says, *"But for the cowardly and unbelieving and abominable and murderers and immoral persons and sorcerers and idolaters and all liars, their part will be in the lake that burns with fire and brimstone, which is the second death."* And finally, look at Matthew 25:46: *"These will go away into eternal punishment, but the righteous into eternal life."* I want to stress that hell is eternal, and anyone who refuses to believe in Jesus will join Satan in hell.

The words for *eternal punishment* in Greek are *kolasin aiōnion*. This word for *punishment, kólasis,* "describes the fearful spirit of the unconverted. Such people never truly embrace the love of God and hence die in the torment of meeting Him only as their Judge rather than their Savior!" [7] Whether we see Jesus as our Savior or our Judge depends on whether or not we put our faith in His work on the cross.

The word for *torment, kolasis,* in Matthew 25:46, refers to "the product of wrong fear about God. A person uses this fear to justify avoiding fellowship with the Lord, finding following Him and His will to be undesirable. This brings on the dread of God's upcoming judgment. An improper fear, or fright, of God also breeds self-condemnation and keeps a person an arm's length from God." [7]

How does God want us to fear him properly? 1 John 4:18 says, *"There is no fear in love; but perfect love casts out fear, because fear involves punishment, and the one who fears is not perfected in love."* I believe John is saying that we should fear God out of our reverent love for Him, which comes from understanding His great love for us as represented by the greatest act of love, the death of Jesus Christ.

The Apostle Paul said in Romans 5:8-11, *"But God demonstrates His own love toward us, in that while we were yet sinners, Christ died for us. Much more then, having now been justified by His blood, we shall be saved from the wrath of God through Him. For if while we were enemies we were reconciled to God through the death of His Son, much more, having been reconciled, we shall be saved by His life. And not only this, but we also exult in God through our Lord Jesus Christ, through whom we have now received the reconciliation."*

This is why we need Jesus. Jesus is the reason we have hope. He died for us so that we can be reconciled to God through Him. Once we have this hope, we no longer have to fear death because we can be confident that our physical death leads to eternal life with Jesus in Heaven! We have no reason to fear because perfect love casts out fear. Jesus is our perfect love.

Have you reached the point of understanding why our faith in Jesus is so important? Today is the day to be saved; we aren't guaranteed tomorrow. If you don't know Jesus as your personal Savior yet, you may be asking yourself, "How do I become saved?" I am glad you asked.

Paul, in Romans 10:8-10, says, *"But what does it say? 'THE WORD IS NEAR YOU, IN YOUR MOUTH AND IN YOUR HEART' — that is, the word of faith which we are preaching, that if you confess with your mouth Jesus as Lord, and believe in your heart that God raised Him from the dead, you will be saved; for with the heart a person believes, resulting in righteousness, and with the mouth he confesses, resulting in salvation."* Today's prayer will be a prayer for salvation.

Pray the prayer for today with all of your heart, and truly believe these words deep in your heart. If you do this, you are now saved! You have been made a new creation in Jesus

Christ. Paul said in 2 Corinthians 5:17-21, *"Therefore if anyone is in Christ, he is a new creature; the old things passed away; behold, new things have come. Now all these things are from God, who reconciled us to Himself through Christ and gave us the ministry of reconciliation, namely, that God was in Christ reconciling the world to Himself, not counting their trespasses against them, and He has committed to us the word of reconciliation. Therefore, we are ambassadors for Christ, as though God were making an appeal through us; we beg you on behalf of Christ, be reconciled to God. He made Him who knew no sin to be sin on our behalf, so that we might become the righteousness of God in Him."*

Now that we have accepted Jesus into our hearts, we must learn to follow Jesus. Tomorrow's question will be, "How do I follow Jesus?"

> *Before proceeding to the next section, review and ask yourself the self-reflection questions listed in the "How to Use This Devotional" section at the beginning of this book.*

# Day 8 Prayer

Father God, today, I learned that I am separated from you because I am a sinner. I acknowledge all of my sins before You, God, and I agree with You that I have fallen short of Your glory. Please, God, give me Your grace and mercy that You promised You would give me. Jesus is Your Son who died on the cross for me so that He could pay the cost for my sin. I believe this, God, with all my heart. You say in Your Word that If I acknowledge with my mouth that Jesus is Lord and believe in my heart that God raised Him from the dead, I will be saved. Jesus is my Lord, and I believe that God raised Him from the dead so that my sins can be forgiven. Thank you, Father, for loving me even when I didn't deserve Your love. Thank you for sending Your Son Jesus to die for me. Thank you, Jesus, for loving me enough to sacrifice Yourself so that I can restore my relationship with You and Your Father. Father, I want to submit myself to You so I can live a holy life set apart for pleasing You and bringing You all the glory, honor, and praise that You and only You deserve. You, Father, have saved my life for eternity, and I am and will always be thankful to You for that. I pray these things in Your Son, Jesus', Mighty name, Amen.

# Day 8 Bible Study Questions

Read John chapter 8 and answer the following questions:

1. Why did they ask Jesus what He thinks they should do with the woman accused of adultery?
    a. What did Jesus say to them after they persisted?
    b. What did the scribes and Pharisees do in response to Jesus' statement?
    c. What did Jesus say to the woman after they had all left?
    d. What character trait does this show in Jesus?
2. Who did Jesus say He was?
    a. After the Pharisees disputed His testimony, why did Jesus say His testimony was true?
    b. Where do you think Jesus was saying He was going?
    c. On who's initiative did Jesus say He was speaking?
3. What did Jesus say they had to do to keep from dying in their sins?
    a. What effect does Jesus say that sin caused a person to experience?
    b. How does one become free from the slavery of sin?
    c. Who does Jesus say the scribes and Pharisees' father was?
    d. Why do you think He says that?

# Day 9: How Do I Follow Jesus?

Now that you have been born again and reconciled to God through the blood of Jesus Christ, you may be asking, "What do I do now? I want to follow Jesus, but I don't know how." I know exactly how you feel. I felt the same way for many years. My friend, Harold, who is teaching me discipleship training, told me, "We have to want what God wants." What does this mean? What does God want?

Micah 6:8 says: *"He has told you, O man, what is good; And what does the Lord require of you but to do justice, to love kindness, and to walk humbly with your God?"* Let's take some time to find the true meaning of this verse.

First, let's look at the phrase *"He has told you, O man."* The word *told* in Hebrew is *nāgaḏ*, which means "He reveals His word as an important report that requires a response which He sets before someone and is undeniable and cannot be ignored." [1] Think of it as God's revelation to you. What has He revealed?

The answer to this question is found in the last part of this verse, *"what is good."* Now let's look deeper into the meaning of the word *good*. The Hebrew word for *good*, *ṭôḇ*, means "a good thing, superior to other choices or options. Preeminently used of the benefits from knowing and obeying the Lord, the only one who is absolutely and intrinsically good." [2] According to God, what is good? God is the only one who is truly good.

Jesus Himself acknowledged this truth. Luke 18:18-19 says, *"A ruler questioned Him, saying, 'Good Teacher, what shall I do to inherit eternal life?' And Jesus said to him, 'Why do you call Me good? No one is good except God alone.'"* If Jesus, a part of the essence of God Himself, said God is the only one who is good, then I believe I should listen if I want to be His follower.

Let's move on to the next phrase, *"And what does the Lord require of you but to do justice."* The word used for *Lord* here is *Yahweh*, the name God gave Himself; *I am that I am.* What does He require of us? To do justice. We understand justice from a human perspective, but what does justice mean to God?

The Hebrew word for *justice, mishpāt,* means "a judgment or God's 'yes' or 'no' verdict. The Lord shares His verdicts (judgments) continuously with receptive believers. This happens by imparting faith (His persuasion) in them which determines the eternal morality of each scene of their life. Justice is supremely used of God's judgments which are based only on the morality of His eternal Being." [3]

From God's perspective, justice is what He determines is right or wrong. Not the world, not ourselves, but Him and Him alone. As we grow in our knowledge of Him, He imparts faith in us and directs us in every scene of our life. As believers who are truly seeking after God's own heart, we are participating with Him in the plan He has for us, allowing Him to be the director of our lives. This takes the pressure off us and puts it on Him.

Jesus says in Matthew 11:29-30, *"Take My yoke upon you and learn from Me, for I am gentle and humble in heart, and YOU WILL FIND REST FOR YOUR SOULS. For My yoke is easy and My burden is light."* Jesus wants us to share our burdens with Him so He can lighten our loads in this life.

The next phrase we will look at is *"to love kindness."* How does the Lord view kindness? In scripture, the word used for *kindness* is *ḥesed*. It means "covenant-loyalty, preeminently, God's perfect loyalty to His covenant. It has often been translated 'mercy' or 'lovingkindness.' But the essence of the term is 'loyalty to God's covenant.'" [4] God made a covenant with us through Jesus. He won't break that covenant, but He doesn't expect us to break it, either. He wants us to love His covenant. Make it our hearts' desire to fully participate in His covenant with Him.

The last part of the verse we will study deeper is *"and to walk humbly with your God?"* First, I want to discuss the word used for *God, Elōhîm*. This word for *God* "expresses Yahweh is in charge of every circumstance as the Creator, the all-powerful One establishing all the physical scenes of life. This divine title in an emphatic plural in Hebrew to dramatically convey Yahweh as always in charge—whose plan always triumphs!" [5] Let's look at this from a human example.

Let's say you work at a large corporation, like Chick-Fil-A. You get hired as a drive-through worker. The corporate CEO of Chick-Fil-A makes a personal visit to your restaurant to see how things are going. He walks up to you and asks you to walk with him and help him understand what's going on in your store to make things better. He didn't choose the owner, the store manager, or even your shift leader. He chose you, someone insignificant in the daily management of the business. You just work there. How would that make you feel about the CEO? That is what God wants to do with us. Knowing that we have nothing to offer Him but our loyalty, He chooses us to help Him run His Kingdom! Isn't that amazing?

Let's continue. The Hebrew word for *walk, halak*, means "to proceed, taking the needed action step(s), intentionally to the next place or stage (destination). Moving on and walking forward with necessary effort toward the resultant progress. It is the verb most frequently employed to describe the act or process of living." [6] God wants us to move forward with Him. But He describes the way we should move — humbly.

The Hebrew word for *humbly*, *şāna'*, means "be modest reflecting God's standards as 'modestly humble' free from inflated, egotistical behavior." [7] In other words, walk with God, being thankful for the opportunity, not prideful because you are special.

Let's put all these three words together in the context of the phrase. God wants us to move forward in our relationship with Him, being thankful for the opportunity and learning to rely on Him to direct our steps by seeking a closer, more personal relationship with Him. How do we draw ourselves closer to God? That will be tomorrow's discussion.

> *Before proceeding to the next section, review and ask yourself the self-reflection questions listed in the "How to Use This Devotional" section at the beginning of this book.*

# Day 9 Prayer

"O Lord, our Lord, how majestic is Your name in all the earth, who have displayed Your splendor above the heavens! From the mouth of infants and nursing babes You have established strength because of Your adversaries, to make the enemy and the revengeful cease. When I consider Your heavens, the work of Your fingers, the moon and the stars, which You have ordained; who am I that You take thought of me and care for me? Yet, You have made me a little lower than God, and You crown me with glory and majesty! You make me to rule over the works of Your hands; You have put all things under my feet, all sheep and oxen, and also the beasts of the field, the birds of the heavens and the fish of the sea, whatever passes through the paths of the seas. O Lord, our Lord, how majestic is Your name in all the earth!" [8] Thank You, Lord, for Your mercy and lovingkindness. Thank You for wanting me to walk with You during the rest of my life for all of eternity. Thank You for making the way for me to know You intimately through Your Son, Jesus! I love You, Lord, with all my heart, all my mind, and all my soul! I pray these words to You in Jesus' Name, Amen.

# Day 9 Bible Study Questions

Read John chapter 9 and answer the following questions:

1.  Why did the disciples think the man was born blind?
    a.  Why did Jesus say the man was born blind?
    b.  What did Jesus do for the man?
2.  Why were the Pharisees angry about the healing of the blind man?
3.  Why were the blind man's parents afraid of saying how he came to see?
4.  Think about the testimony the blind man gave about Jesus. Why do you think the Pharisees got upset about it and put the man out?
5.  Why did Jesus say that He came into the world?
6.  What do you think Jesus means by saying, "so that those who do not see may see, and that those who see may become blind?"

# Day 10: How Do I Draw Myself Closer to God?

In yesterday's discussion, I shared that following Jesus means we must want what God wants. I discussed how Micah 6:8 describes what God wants for us. It says, *"to do justice, to love kindness, and to walk humbly with your God."* I broke down these three phrases and explained in detail what they mean.

Let's put them together in one explanation to get the big picture. This verse means we should seek to do what God says is right and turn from what He says is wrong through the faith He imparts in us as we seek Him. We need to make it our hearts' desire to participate fully in the covenant He has made with us and move forward in our relationship with Him, being thankful that we get the opportunity to participate with Him to build His Kingdom. We do this knowing that He directs our steps as we draw ourselves into a more intimate relationship with Him. This is what He says is good, to know Him and obey Him.

How do we do that? Jesus tells us how to do that. Remember in John 14:6 when Jesus says, *"I am the way, and the truth and the life. No one comes to the Father but through Me."* Jesus Himself is the road map to how we draw closer to God, His Father. When we get to know Jesus, we get to know God. Why? Because Jesus is God.

In John 14:7, Jesus continues, *"If you had known Me, you*

*would have known my Father also; from now on you know Him, and have seen Him."* Jesus is telling His disciples that by knowing Him, they know the Father because they are part of the same Essence. But His disciples didn't understand what He was telling them. Look at what Philip asked Jesus in John 14:8: *"Philip said to Him, 'Lord, show us the Father, and it is enough for us.'"*

Jesus answers Philip in John 14:9-11. *"Jesus said to him, 'Have I been so long with you, and yet you have not come to know Me, Philip? He who has seen Me has seen the Father; how can you say, 'Show us the Father'? Do you not believe that I am in the Father, and the Father is in Me? The words that I say to you I do not speak on My own initiative, but the Father abiding in Me does His works. Believe Me that I am in the Father and the Father is in Me; otherwise believe because of the works themselves.'"*

What Jesus is saying here is very important. Jesus is explaining to them how He and His Father are in perfect relationship. Let's examine this closely. First, Jesus asks Philip, *"Have I been so long with you, and yet you have not come to know me?"*

To understand why Jesus is asking this question, we have to look closer at the timing of this event. This is a part of the last recorded conversation Jesus has with His disciples before He is taken off to be executed on the cross. Jesus had been with Philip and His other disciples twenty-four-seven for over three years. During this time, they had seen Jesus perform miracles, healing, and even a couple of resurrections. Jesus had been teaching them many things that no one had ever taught, such as Jesus saying here that He is in the Father and the Father is in Him.

What does this mean for us? It means that we can know who Jesus is and still not truly know Him. Jesus is trying to help His disciples understand this point. Essentially, Jesus is saying to them, "After all you have seen and heard, how do you not recognize me already as Immanuel, or God with us?" Jesus wants them to have this close intimate relationship with Him, so He is giving them the intimate details about His relationship with His Father. Do you know *about* Jesus, or do you know Jesus *personally*?

The next question Jesus asks Philip is, *"He who has seen Me has seen the Father; how can you say, 'Show us the Father'?"* In Matthew 16:15-16, Jesus asked His disciples, *"But who do you say that I am?" Simon Peter answered, "You are the Christ, the Son of the Living God."* Peter had properly answered Jesus' question in front of all His disciples. Yet, Philip, and possibly others, still didn't truly understand.

The next question Jesus asked Philip was, *"Do you not believe that I am in the Father, and the Father is in Me?"* I believe Jesus isn't asking this question to reprimand Philip but to make him think. This is hard for us to understand because it references part of the Trinity of God. I believe this is Jesus' method to get them to start thinking differently because He was about to tell them the truth.

The next statement Jesus made is critical to understand. He says, *"The words that I say to you I do not speak on My own initiative, but the Father abiding in Me does His works."* Jesus is telling them that everything He has said and done was in full obedience to the work of His Father, who lives in Him. He is teaching them by example how to fully submit their lives to God by following His will.

Jesus' last statement in John 14:9-11 was, *"Believe Me that I am in the Father and the Father is in Me; otherwise believe because of the works themselves."* Jesus is giving them a choice. He says you can either believe this because I am telling you this, or you can believe because of the works you have seen me do.

Now let's look at the next few verses. John 14:12-15 says, *"Truly, truly, I say to you, he who believes in Me, the works that*

*I do, he will do also; and greater works than these he will do; because I go to the Father. Whatever you ask in My name, that will I do, so that the Father may be glorified in the Son. If you ask Me anything in My name, I will do it. If you love Me, you will keep My commandments."*

Jesus is first explaining to them that anyone who believes in Jesus and His works, they will do works for the Kingdom as well, some even greater than Jesus did. He then explains that if they ask for anything that brings the Father glory in Jesus' name, He will do it for them. Finally, Jesus is telling them how to show Him they love Him by doing what He told them to do.

The word for *commandments* used here is *entolē*. It means *"'in the end,' focusing on the end-result (objective) of a command."* [1] Jesus is telling us that we shouldn't do what He says out of fear of punishment but rather out of an expression of love towards Him, looking forward to the day we will see Him again.

We draw ourselves closer to God by learning more about Jesus. How do we do that? We learn about Him by reading the Bible, which is the Word of God. Think back to what we learned earlier in John 1:1: *"In the beginning was the Word, the Word was God and the Word was with God."* John describes Jesus here as being the Word of God. The Bible is the Word of God, the story of Jesus from the beginning to the end.

In my testimony, I said that during my time fasting and seeking Jesus in the Bible that I had finally met Jesus. This was true because I had read His story for the first time in my life. You may say, "I have read the Bible, but I don't feel like I have met Jesus." Here is a question to ask yourself. "Why was I reading the Bible?"

Were you reading the Bible out of a sense of obligation? *I am doing this because it's what my pastor says I should do.* Or were you reading the Bible out of a desire to know Jesus?

While reading the Bible during my fast, I wanted to know who Jesus was. I wanted to meet Jesus. And remember, Jesus said to His disciples, *"If you ask Me anything in My name, I will do it."* [2] Have you ever read the Bible after asking Jesus to reveal Himself to you?

Tomorrow, we will continue to study John chapter 14, picking up where we left off. Jesus tells His disciples more about what will happen after He leaves them. He will send them the Spirit of Truth, or the Holy Spirit. Tomorrow our question will be, "Who is the Holy Spirit?"

---

*Before proceeding to the next section, review and ask yourself the self-reflection questions listed in the "How to Use This Devotional" section at the beginning of this book.*

# Day 10 Prayer

Father God, today, I learned how to draw myself closer to You. Father, to do that, I have to learn more about Your Son, Jesus. Father, Jesus said He is the only way I have to get to You. I believe Him. Jesus said that He abides in You and You in Him. I believe Him. Father, help me to want what You want. Help me to learn what it is You say is right and help me to have the desire to do those things. Help me learn what You say is wrong and remove any desire to do those things. Father, I want to know You and Your Son more intimately. I want to learn how to be in a closer relationship with You. "Make me know Your ways, O Lord; teach me Your paths. Lead me in Your truth and teach me, for You are the God of my salvation; For You, I wait all the day. Remember, O Lord, Your compassion and Your lovingkindness, for they have been from of old. Do not remember the sins of my youth or my transgressions; according to Your lovingkindness remember me, for Your goodness' sake, O Lord. Good and upright is the Lord; therefore, He instructs sinners in the way. He leads the humble in justice, and He teaches the humble His way. All the paths of the Lord are lovingkindness and truth to those who keep His covenant and His testimonies. For Your name's sake, O Lord, pardon my iniquity, for it is great." [3] I ask all of these things in Jesus' Mighty Name, Amen.

# Day 10 Bible Study Questions

Read John chapter 10 and answer the following questions:

1. In John 10:1, where do you think the door leads to that Jesus is referring to? Hint: John 14:6.
   a. Who does Jesus say the doorkeeper is?
   b. Where does the door lead to?
2. What role does Jesus say that the Good Shepherd has?
3. Who do you think the other sheep are that Jesus is referring to? Hint: at this moment, Jesus is speaking to the Jews.
4. In verses 22-30, what is Jesus saying about Himself?
5. Why were the Jews trying to stone Jesus?
6. What did Jesus tell them He did that showed them He was telling the truth?

# Day 11: Who is the Holy Spirit?

Today, we will discuss the third person of God, the Holy Spirit. We have learned that the Holy Spirit was present with God from the beginning, just like Jesus. He is also a part of the Essence of God, equally God but with a different purpose than God and Jesus. What purpose does the Holy Spirit have as part of the Godhead?

The Holy Spirit came upon Jesus as He was baptized by John the Baptist. Matthew 3:16-17 reads, *"After being baptized, Jesus came up immediately from the water; and behold, the heavens were opened, and he saw the Spirit of God descending as a dove and lighting on Him, and behold, a voice out of the heavens said, 'This is My beloved Son, in whom I am well-pleased.'"* I believe this happened not because Jesus needed the Holy Spirit to communicate with God Himself, but as an example to show us that we need the Holy Spirit to communicate with God.

The Bible describes several roles of the Holy Spirit. A few of them are a Helper, a Teacher, a Convictor of sin, and a Giver of knowledge or wisdom from God. Let's continue where we left off in John chapter 14 from yesterday. Jesus told His disciples that He was in the Father, and the Father was in Him. And He said that all the work He did was from His Father's initiative. Next, He told His disciples something they had never heard before.

In John 14:16-17, Jesus says, *"I will ask the Father, and He will give you another Helper, that He may be with you forever; that is the Spirit of truth, whom the world cannot receive, because it does not see Him or know Him, but you know Him because He abides with you and will be in you."* Jesus tells them that soon He will send them a Helper and calls Him the Spirit of Truth.

The word *Helper* in Greek is *paráklētos*. It means "a legal advocate, literally one who makes the right judgment-call because He is close enough to the situation. Helper is used of the Holy Spirit and Christ, our heavenly advocates who continuously work on our behalf. They offer up the evidence that stands up in the court of heaven!" [1]

Jesus said this Helper, or Spirit of truth, abides with us and will be in us. Jesus sends a legal advocate to dwell in us when we surrender our lives to Him in faith. As we seek this close, personal relationship with God through Jesus, we are given this Spirit, who helps us make the right decisions God wants us to make. How amazing is that!

The next purpose of the Holy Spirit is our Teacher. Let's look at what Jesus says next about the Holy Spirit to His disciples. In John 14:25-26, Jesus says, *"These things I have spoken to you while abiding with you. But the Helper, the Holy Spirit, whom the Father will send in My name, He will teach you all things, and bring to your remembrance all that I said to you."* Jesus speaks again of the Helper, calling Him the Holy Spirit. He says He is our Teacher and will remind us what Jesus tells us from the Word.

Think back to my testimony for a minute. The first time I ever heard the Holy Spirit speak to me was when I decided to start fasting and read the book about Revelation. He told me to stop reading the book and read the gospels. I obeyed Him. When I did, I had a personal experience with Jesus. This was the Holy Spirit acting for me as a Helper and a Teacher showing me how to find Jesus.

The next purpose of the Holy Spirit is to convict us of our sin. Let's look at John 16:7-11. *"But I tell you the truth, it is to your advantage that I go away; for if I do not go away, the Helper will not come to you; but if I go, I will send Him to you. And He, when He comes, will convict the world concerning sin and righteousness and judgment; concerning sin, because they do not believe in Me; and concerning righteousness, because I go to the Father and you no longer see Me; and concerning judgment, because the ruler of this world has been judged."*

Jesus describes three areas of conviction in which the Holy Spirit is involved: sin, righteousness, and judgment. Let's discuss each of these to be sure we understand each area carefully.

The word used for *sin* is *hamartia*. It means "missing the mark." [2] Jesus says the judgment concerning sin is because they do not believe in Him. This falls in line with the judgment Jesus speaks of in John 3:18: *"He who does not believe has been judged already, because he has not believed in the name of the only begotten Son of God."* What is Jesus saying by making these two statements about sin in agreement with each other?

While it's true that God gave Moses the law to make us aware that we are sinners, the law itself isn't what condemns us to hell. It's our unwillingness to believe in Jesus as the Son of God, who died to save us from our sins. This is what condemns us. It doesn't really matter what we do before we put our faith in Jesus; we are already eternally separated from God, facing the judgment of hell. The only thing that saves us from judgment is putting our faith in Jesus. Don't misunderstand what I am saying. God can't be in the presence of sin and doesn't want us to sin because that is disobedience to Him. But Jesus is the only way that we can overcome our sin and present ourselves as righteous before God.

Next, let's look at the conviction of righteousness. The word used for *righteousness* is *dikaiosýnē*. It means simply "the approval of God." [3] How do conviction and righteousness go together? To understand, we have to look at the true meaning of conviction. The word used for *conviction* is *elégxō*. It means "to convince by solid, compelling evidence which especially exposes what is wrong or right." [4] Jesus is saying we can have confidence in conviction of righteousness because He will be raised from the dead and be with God in Heaven as our Advocate.

Jesus also says that the Holy Spirit will help convince us with solid evidence to know if we are in right standing with God. If you have any doubt about whether or not you are saved, I suggest praying to God and asking the Holy Spirit to search your heart and help you discover where that doubt comes from so you can work it out.

The next purpose of the Holy Spirit is to impart to us the knowledge or wisdom of God. The first knowledge we get is truth. Look at what Jesus says in John 16:13-15: *"But when He, the Spirit of truth, comes, He will guide you into all the truth; for He will not speak on His own initiative, but whatever He hears, He will speak; and He will disclose to you what is to come. He will glorify Me, for He will take of Mine and will disclose it to you. All things that the Father has are Mine; therefore, I said that He takes of Mine and will disclose it to you."*

Here Jesus is saying that the Holy Spirit will help lead us to the truth. Who did we establish was the truth? Jesus is the truth. The Holy Spirit's job is to help us know Jesus. If you are reading the Bible, seeking Jesus, and having a hard time, pray to God and ask Him to help you understand. This will be pleasing to God because it's His will for you to want to know Him.

But there is also the knowledge the Holy Spirit gives us to help us carry out God's will for our lives. Exodus 31:1-5 says, *"Now the Lord spoke to Moses, saying, 'See, I have called by name Bezalel, the son of Uri, the son of Hur, of the tribe of Judah. And I have filled him with the Spirit of God in wisdom, in understanding, in knowledge, and in all kinds of craftsmanship, to make artistic designs for work in gold, in silver, and in bronze, and in the cutting of stones for settings, and in the carving of wood, that he may work in all kinds of craftsmanship.'"* God set the Holy Spirit upon this man to give Him the knowledge and skill needed to build the tabernacle and the instruments God wanted to be made for the sacrifice.

The Holy Spirit is the part of God that gives us His power to do His will in our lives. God wants us to bring Him all of the glory. He uses our weakness to show His strength when He uses us to help Him build His Kingdom on Earth.

Now that we know more about the third part of the Trinity of God, the Holy Spirit, tomorrow, we will look into how it all comes together for our good. The question we will discuss tomorrow is, "How do I teach my heart to want what God wants?"

*Before proceeding to the next section, review and ask yourself the self-reflection questions listed in the "How to Use This Devotional" section at the beginning of this book.*

# Day 11 Prayer

Father God, today, I learned more about the third part of Your Essence, the Holy Spirit. Father, I learned that before Jesus rose to be in Heaven with You, He made me a promise. The promise was that He wouldn't leave me alone. He would send me a Helper, the Holy Spirit, that would dwell in me forever as a sign that Jesus would one day return to establish His kingdom here on Earth. Father, I thank you for that.

Thank you, Father, for loving me enough to be with me while I am facing life's difficulties while waiting on Jesus' return. Thank you for giving me a teacher to help me learn about Jesus as I seek Him in the Word. Thank you for loving me so much that You won't leave me where I am. You are perfecting me by Your blood shed for me on the cross and Your resurrection three days later so that when You return, I will stand before You, wearing Your righteousness that only comes from Your blood. The Holy Spirit helps me by telling me when I am doing wrong in Your eyes so I can turn from my sin. He also helps me by giving me the confidence that I am Yours now. Because He is in me, I know that Jesus is with You in Heaven as my Advocate.

Lastly, Father, thank You for giving me the Holy Spirit so that I can share in the knowledge that You want me to have to do Your good works for the Kingdom of God. I don't deserve that, but You gave me Your mercy and grace anyway. As I learn to want what You want, fill me with Your Spirit and teach me how to do that. I am asking You, Father, all these things in Jesus' Mighty Name, Amen!

# Day 11 Bible Study Questions

Read John chapter 11 and answer the following questions:

1. How does John say that Jesus felt about Lazarus?
2. What did Jesus say that Lazarus' sickness would be used for?
3. Why did Jesus stay two more days before leaving?
4. Why did Thomas say they should go with Him?
    a. What do you think He meant by that?
5. What was Lazarus' condition when Jesus found Him?
    a. Why was this important?
6. What did Jesus want to show His disciples?
7. What did Jesus do when He saw Mary and Martha weeping?
8. What did Jesus do for Lazarus?
9. What did the chief priests and Pharisees want to do to Jesus?
    a. What did they have planned?

# Day 12: How Do I Teach My Heart to Want What God Wants?

As we learn to be disciples of Jesus, committed, lifelong learners and followers of Jesus, we have learned that we must want what God wants. How do we do that exactly? We must learn to look at things from God's perspective, not our own.

God wants us to turn from our sinful ways and start living in the abundant way He created us to live. While we can only stop sinning by the power of the Holy Spirit, what about the corruption sin has placed in our hearts and minds? How do we learn to see our sin as God sees it?

Before I get into teaching again, I want to take some time to go back over a part of my testimony that is important to understand. As you recall, my three-month fasting period led me to the first personal encounter with Jesus I had ever had. And while I had met Jesus, I didn't learn to see the sin in my life the way God wanted me to see it. How I viewed my video game habit didn't change. Why? Because I wasn't ready at that time to give my life fully to Jesus.

In Luke 9:23-24, Jesus tells His disciples, *"If anyone wishes to come after Me, he must deny himself, and take up his cross daily and follow Me. For whoever wishes to save his life will lose it, but whoever loses his life for My sake, he is the one who will save it."* Truly following Jesus comes at a cost. We must be willing to give up anything we are living for in this world and start living in full obedience to Jesus' instructions.

At that time, I wasn't ready to fully give up my desire to play video games and follow Jesus. I wasn't able to see my video game habit as an addiction. We have identified that idolatry is the proper label for the sin of addiction. I was still loving something more than Jesus. I didn't see the sin in my life as God wanted me to see it. Praise be to God that He wasn't done with me yet. Jesus showed me the truth about my sin through the Holy Spirit we discussed yesterday, and He saved my life forever.

What Jesus is saying in Luke is that to truly follow Him, we must be willing to fully submit ourselves to Him. It doesn't mean that we change all at once. It means that we must be willing to be honest with ourselves by searching our hearts to let the Holy Spirit cut out any sin that we are holding on to. This process is called *sanctification*. Sanctification happens from the time of salvation until the time of *glorification*. Glorification occurs when we have put our faith in Jesus and died or when Jesus has returned.

In Luke 12:2-5, Jesus says, *"But there is nothing covered up that will not be revealed, and hidden that will not be known. Accordingly, whatever you have said in the dark will be heard in the light, and what you have whispered in the inner rooms will be proclaimed upon the housetops.*

*"I say to you, My friends, do not be afraid of those who kill the body and after that have no more that they can do. But I will warn you whom to fear: fear the One who, after He has killed, has authority to cast into hell; yes, I tell you, fear Him!"*

It may be hard for us to admit, but there is nothing, let me repeat that, nothing we can do that God doesn't know about, whether it's something we do, a thought we have, or a desire in our hearts. Let's look at a few verses about how God sees the heart.

Genesis 6:5 says, *"Then the Lord saw that the wickedness of man was great on the earth, and that every intent of the thoughts of his heart was only evil continually."* I want to shed some light on the original meanings of the words *heart* and *evil*. First, I want to look at the word *heart* since it's so important to God. The Hebrew word for *heart* is *lēb*. It is "the seat of moral preference and thought. It includes 'inner thinking' which both precedes and works out behavior. Also, the heart is the seat of our deepest inclinations, resolutions, appetites, will, passions – as one thinks and feels in the inner man." [1]

The Hebrew word used for evil is *ra'*, which primarily means "what causes pain." [2] The intention of their thoughts or their deepest inclinations caused continual pain. Think about that for a minute; let it sink in. Every thought they had was intended to cause themselves or others pain. If you haven't read the book of Genesis before, God said this right before He sent the flood to destroy all mankind except Noah, his wife, sons, and daughters-in-law. [3] God takes seriously people hurting His children.

Psalms 44:21 says, *"Would not God find this out? For He knows the secrets of the heart."* This verse, along with Genesis 6:5, shows that God knows everything about us at all times. When God says we should repent and confess our sins to Him, it's not because He doesn't know about our sins. He wants us to come to Him humbly in agreement with Him to tell Him that we understand that what we did was wrong in His eyes. Are we only confessing our sins in an attempt to get forgiveness from God? If we do this but don't fully agree with Him that the sin is wrong, we merely give Him lip service. What God wants most from us is a changed heart.

Proverbs 28:26 says, *"He who trusts in his own HEART is a fool, but he who walks wisely will be delivered."* And Jeremiah 17:9-10 says, *"The heart is more deceitful than all else and is desperately sick; who can understand it? I, the Lord, search the heart, I test the mind, even to give to each man according to his ways, according to the results of his deeds."*

I have come to understand this over the past four years of desperately seeking God. I look back over my adult life, and it was a wreck for the twenty-five years I wasn't seeking God. I, on my own understanding, can't trust myself to do good. The only way I can be sure that I am doing good is by seeking God and relying on His Word to determine what good is and then doing it.

In Mark 7:20-23, Jesus says, *"That which proceeds out of the man, that is what defiles the man. For from within, out of the heart of men, proceed the evil thoughts, fornications, thefts, murders, adulteries, deeds of coveting and wickedness, as well as deceit, sensuality, envy, slander, pride and foolishness. All these evil things proceed from within and defile the man."* Jesus says that man alone, relying on his understanding, can't do good. Sometimes we coincidentally do things that align with what God says is good. But there is a popular quote, "Even a broken clock is right twice a day."

Deuteronomy 11:13-21 says, *"And it shall come about, if you listen obediently to my commandments which I am commanding you today, to love the Lord your God and to serve Him with all your heart and all your soul, that He will give the rain for your land in its season, the early and late rain, that you may gather in your grain and your new wine and your oil. And He will give grass in your fields for your cattle, and you shall eat and be satisfied. Beware, lest your hearts be deceived and you turn away and serve other gods and worship them. Or the anger of the Lord will be kindled against you, and He will shut up the heavens so that there will be no rain and the ground will not yield its fruit; and you will perish quickly from the good land which the Lord is giving you.*

*"You shall therefore impress these words of mine on your heart and on your soul; and you shall bind them as a sign on your hand, and they shall be as frontals on your forehead. And you shall teach them to your sons, talking of them when you sit in your*

*house and when you walk along the road and when you lie down and when you rise up. And you shall write them on the doorposts of your house and on your gates, so that your days and the days of your sons may be multiplied on the land which the Lord swore to your fathers to give them, as long as the heavens remain above the earth."*

This is what God wants for us, to give Him our WHOLE heart. Not fifty percent, seventy-five percent, or even ninety percent. One hundred percent of our hearts is what He wants. When we put Him in the proper place in our hearts, He blesses us. But when we don't, He curses us. Then He says we should do whatever it takes for us to remind ourselves of how much we need Him.

Deuteronomy 10:16 says, *"Circumcise then your heart, and stiffen your neck no more."* The word *circumcise* means to remove the sin from your heart. To do this, we have to search our hearts while seeking in the Bible the truth of what we should do. As we learn what God says is right, we should start doing those things. As we learn what God says is wrong, we should stop doing those things. This is the process of training our hearts to want what God wants. We will discuss tomorrow the question, "How do I circumcise my heart?"

This is eight of the six-hundred-seventy-five times the word heart is mentioned in the New American Standard Version of the Bible. I believe if God refers to the heart that many times in His Word, we need to spend some time searching our own.

*Before proceeding to the next section, review and ask yourself the self-reflection questions listed in the "How to Use This Devotional" section at the beginning of this book.*

# Day 12 Prayer

Father God, I learned today that there is evil in my heart that I have not addressed. Father, I need You to search my heart and reveal any wicked ways You find. "Have mercy upon me, O God, according to Your lovingkindness; according to the multitude of Your tender mercies, blot out my transgressions. Wash me thoroughly from my iniquity, and cleanse me from my sin. For I acknowledge my transgressions, and my sin is always before me. Against You, You only, have I sinned, and done this evil in Your sight that You may be found just when You speak, and blameless when You judge. Behold, I was brought forth in iniquity, and in sin my mother conceived me. Behold, You desire truth in the inward parts, and in the hidden part You will make me to know wisdom. Purge me with hyssop, and I shall be clean; wash me, and I shall be whiter than snow. Make me hear joy and gladness, that the bones You have broken may rejoice. Hide Your face from my sins, and blot out all my iniquities. Create in me a clean heart, O God, and renew a steadfast spirit within me. Do not cast me away from Your presence, and do not take Your Holy Spirit from me. Restore to me the joy of Your salvation, and uphold me by Your generous Spirit. Then I will teach transgressors Your ways, and sinners shall be converted to You. Deliver me from the guilt of my sin, O God, The God of my salvation, and my tongue shall sing aloud of Your righteousness. O Lord, open my lips, and my mouth shall show forth Your praise. For You do not desire sacrifice, or else I would give it; You do not delight in burnt offering. The sacrifices of God are a broken spirit, a broken and a contrite heart. These, O God, You will not despise." [4] Father, I pray to you these things in Jesus' Mighty Name, Amen!

# Day 12 Bible Study Questions

Read John chapter 12 and answer the following questions:

1. When Mary anointed the feet of Jesus with the perfume, why did Judas Iscariot get upset?
    a. What do you think Judas would have done with the money had the perfume been sold?
    b. Why did Jesus say Mary was anointing Him?
2. Why did the chief priests want to kill Lazarus along with Jesus?
3. How did Jesus enter Jerusalem?
    a. What was the significance of His entrance on a donkey?
4. Why were the people following after Jesus? (Verse 18)
5. In verse 25, what do you think Jesus means by "he who loves his life loses it?"
    a. What about "he who hates his life in this world will keep it to life eternal?"
6. Why did Jesus say to the crowd the voice came out of heaven?
    a. Whose voice do you think it was?
    b. What did He say?
7. What was Jesus telling them was about to happen to Him?
8. Why were people who believed Jesus not confessing Him?
9. What will judge people who do not believe in Jesus on the last day?

# Day 13: How Do I Circumcise My Heart?

We learned that because of sin, our hearts are full of evil. When we give our lives to Jesus, we are saved from our past sins. But this act doesn't actually change our hearts. So how do we do that?

We search our hearts for what we feel is most important to us. Let me start by asking some questions for you to consider.

1. How do I typically treat the people whom I come into contact with?
2. Do I put what is important to me before what is important to other people?
3. When I wake up in the morning, what is the first thing I think of?
4. What is the last thing I think of when I lay down at night?
5. How do my behaviors look compared to how God says I should act?
6. Do I treat other people how I would want them to treat me?
   a. If not, what should I start to do differently?
7. What are some of the things I couldn't live without?
   a. Why do I think I need them?
8. If my deepest darkest secrets were revealed to the world, how would the world think of me?
   a. How would God think of me?

b.  How would that make me feel?

The questions above are designed to get you thinking about your true heart condition. I want you to write them down, take a screenshot, or do something to have them available to review several times a day throughout the next few days. This will get you to start recognizing what you are thinking about and how you treat others. This will start the process of analyzing your heart. I will be honest, I have had to ask myself and answer most, if not all, of these questions over the past four years. I had to admit to myself some difficult truths about who I was and how I treated others. But in the end, it has led me to a deeper relationship with Jesus.

The question for today is, "How do I circumcise my heart?" The Hebrew word for *circumcise* is *mûl*, which means "to cut away the foreskin of the male organ." [1] This is extra skin that has no real function. God gave the command of circumcision in Genesis 17:10-11. God said, *"This is My covenant, which you shall keep, between Me and you and your descendants after you: every male among you shall be circumcised. And you shall be circumcised in the flesh of your foreskin; and it shall be the sign of the covenant between Me and you."*

"The rite of circumcision was a sign and a seal of the covenant relationship between God and the believer." [2] "Circumcision symbolizes the wonderful opportunity to enter *into covenant relationship* with the Lord, through the *seed* of Messiah. It was a constant reminder that the Israelites were a *chosen seed*, from which Messiah would ultimately spring." [3]

When Jesus came and died for us, He made a new covenant with us: through believing in Him, we would be saved. Jesus' sacrifice fulfilled the old covenant. Now instead of circumcising our foreskin, we circumcise our hearts.

This was the circumcision that God had always wanted from us anyway. Look at what He said in Deuteronomy 30:2-3,6: *"...and you return to the Lord your God and obey Him with all your heart and soul according to all that I command you today, you and your sons, then the Lord your God will restore you from captivity, and have compassion on you, and will gather you again from all the peoples where the Lord your God has scattered you.... Moreover the Lord your God will circumcise your heart and the heart of your descendants, to love the Lord your God with all your heart and with all your soul, in order that you may live."*

This circumcision brings us life. Circumcision of the heart means cutting out the sin in our hearts. Sin has no value at all to God. Then we start doing the things God says we should do. As we do this, we grow deeper and deeper into a more intimate relationship with Jesus.

Over the next few days, we are going to discuss how to circumcise our hearts in detail. We are going to discuss how to put off self by identifying areas in our hearts, minds, and actions that do not align with God's standard and remove them. Then we will discuss how to put on the things God wants us to do to bring Him glory. Today we will focus on why and how we put off self.

The Apostle Paul said in Ephesians 4:20-24, *"But you did not learn Christ in this way, if indeed you have heard Him and have been taught in Him, just as truth is in Jesus, that, in reference to your former manner of life, you lay aside the old self, which is being corrupted in accordance with the lusts of deceit, and that you be renewed in the spirit of your mind, and put on the new self, which in the likeness of God has been created in righteousness and holiness of the truth."*

Paul says since we have been born again in the Spirit, we should seek to live by the Spirit, not by our old fleshly desires. So, we must put off the old self, which is our old habits and sinful ways of thinking, and put on the new self, which is learning and doing what God wants us to do. We do this by being renewed in the spirit of our minds. In Hebrew, they considered the heart and the mind connected, so they didn't use different words to describe them.

How do we start to put off self? We must learn how to think differently about our lives now that we are disciples of Jesus. Look what Paul said in Romans 12:1-3: *"Therefore I urge you, brethren, by the mercies of God, to present your bodies a living and holy sacrifice, acceptable to God, which is your spiritual service of worship. And do not be conformed to this world, but be transformed by the renewing of your mind, so that you may prove what the will of God is, that which is good and acceptable and perfect. For through the grace given to me I say to everyone among you not to think more highly of himself than he ought to think; but to think so as to have sound judgment, as God has allotted to each a measure of faith."*

Paul says we should be transformed by the renewing of our minds. The world around us and the sin in our hearts has corrupted our way of thinking. We believed that the things we were doing were good; otherwise, we wouldn't have been doing them. But God says they aren't good at all. We have to start thinking about things the way God does.

When God created the world, He created it in perfect order and harmony. The devil tricked Adam and Eve into thinking God was telling them a lie or withholding something good from them that wasn't good at all. What was it that was being withheld? The knowledge of good and evil. They learned how to do evil when they disobeyed God's command.

Looking back on some of the decisions I made, I can honestly say that I thought they were good at the time. But they weren't. They were evil. I hurt myself and those around me.

The renewing of our minds leads us to proving what the will of God is, that which is good and acceptable and perfect. Think about that. God wants us to know what is good, what is acceptable to Him, and what is perfect. The Holy Spirit He places in us helps discern the truths from the lies when we ask Him for help and seek the truth in the Bible.

The last part of the above Scripture says we shouldn't think more highly of ourselves than we should. Rather, we should seek to think with the sound judgment God gives us through faith in Him. What is that sound judgment? We should want what God wants for us, not what we want for ourselves.

What is the biggest focus of your life? Do you focus on pleasing yourself? Do you focus on getting the things you want? Do you want people to agree with you and your opinions about life? What is the primary focus of your conversations when you are talking to someone? Do most of your sentences start with you as the subject? Do you focus on how others treat you? If you answered yes to many of these questions, you may be guilty of thinking more highly of yourself than you should. Before becoming a follower of Jesus, I was guilty of answering yes to most of these questions. You are not alone.

Paul said in Romans 8:5-8, *"For those who are according to the flesh set their minds on the things of the flesh, but those who are according to the Spirit, the things of the Spirit. For the mind set on the flesh is death, but the mind set on the Spirit is life and peace, because the mind set on the flesh is hostile toward God; for it does not subject itself to the law of God, for it is not even able to do so, and those who are in the flesh cannot please God."* The question we must ask is, "Do I want to please myself, or do I want to please God?"

---

*Before proceeding to the next section, review and ask yourself the self-reflection questions listed in the "How to Use This Devotional" section at the beginning of this book.*

# Day 13 Prayer

Father God, you say in Your Word, "You who seek God, let your heart revive. For the Lord hears the needy, and does not despise." [3] Father, I desperately need Your help. Do not despise me, Father, but search my heart and reveal any selfish ways I hold on to. I want to learn how to want what You want. I want to put off my old selfish ways and put on the new ways that You say that I should. Father, give me eyes that see, ears that hear Your truth, and a heart that longs for You. Pour Your Spirit upon me so I can learn from You what is good and pleasing to You. Reveal to me the evil that I do so that I can circumcise it from my heart. Teach me Your holy ways, Lord, and do not let me go on sinning against You. My heart grieves the hurt I have caused Your children, Father; please forgive me for all the pain I have caused. Take away my selfish desires of the heart and replace them with what pleases You. I submit it all to You, Father. I pray these things in Jesus' Mighty Name, Amen!

# Day 13 Bible Study Questions

Read John chapter 13 and answer the following questions:

1. How long does it say that Jesus loved His own in the world?
2. Why does John say that Judas betrayed Jesus?
3. What did Jesus get up from the table to do?
4. Why do you think Jesus said, "If I do not wash you, you have no part in Me?"
5. Why did Jesus say that He washed their feet?
6. What do you think is the lesson Jesus is trying to teach them in John 13:12-17?
7. What was the New Commandment Jesus gave them at the table?
8. What did Jesus tell Peter that He would do?
   a. What would happen after Peter did it?

# Day 14: What is Love?

I originally planned to show you how to start cutting out the sin in your heart today. But the Holy Spirit spoke to me and said, "How can you expect someone to reach their destination if they don't know where they are going?" He told me to show you the destination first. The destination is love. God wants us to love others the way He loves us. Before we can do that, we have to understand how to love the way God loves us.

Before we get into defining love, I want you to do something. Get a piece of paper and write down your best definition of love. It doesn't matter what you write as long as it is what you truly believe about love.

The word *love* itself is in the NASB version of the Bible 309 times. This means understanding love is important to God. Jesus told His disciples in John 15:12-13, *"This is My commandment, that you love one another, just as I have loved you. Greater love has no one than this, that one lay down his life for his friends."* Jesus is telling them to love other people the way He loved them. Jesus died for us so that our sins could be washed away and we could be reconciled to God.

I had to ask myself, "If I lay down my life for another person in love, how is that good for the Kingdom of God?" The answer I came upon was this: one sacrificial act of love isn't actually what Jesus wants us to do. He wants us to love other people more than we love this world.

We must look at people the way God sees them. Every person that has ever lived, past, present, and future, is precious in God's eyes. He created us all in His image. He created us to be in a relationship with Him. He created us to love Him and rule over this world with Him. His greatest desire is for us to be reconciled to Him. That's why He put on flesh, as Jesus, and died for us because He loves us [1].

How do we define love the way God sees love? First, we have to look at love in the context of the original language. In English, we have only one word to describe all the different types of love. That isn't true in Greek; multiple words are used to describe love.

The Greek word used to describe love in John 15 is *agapáō*. The word means "a believer choosing to 'live through Christ' embracing His will (choosing His choices) and obeying them through His power." [2] In other words, this love means choosing what God, who is love, prefers. 1 John 4:8 says, *"The one who does not love does not know God, for God is love."* Since God is love, knowing God is the only way to truly express love.

Another definition of agapáō love is "to focus on embracing what God embraces by knowing Him, which (ironically) also includes hating what God hates." [2] Psalms 97:10 says, *"Hate evil, you who love the Lord, who preserves the souls of His godly ones; He delivers them from the hand of the wicked."* Godly love is to protect one from evil and lead one to good, which is God.

This type of love, agapáō, in Scripture is "to act for a person's highest good which is always and only defined (revealed) by the Lord." [2] God expects us to love Him and love others as demonstrated in Mark 12:30-31: *"'AND YOU SHALL LOVE THE LORD YOUR GOD WITH ALL YOUR HEART, AND WITH ALL YOUR SOUL, AND WITH ALL YOUR MIND, AND WITH ALL YOUR STRENGTH.' The second is this, 'YOU SHALL LOVE YOUR NEIGHBOR AS YOURSELF.' There is no other commandment greater than these."*

The Holy Spirit reveals to us how to love this way as we get to know Jesus in the Scriptures. The only way we can truly carry out love in this fashion is to rely on the power of Jesus given to us through the Holy Spirit. This love defies our carnal (sinful) nature to put self before others.

Now go back to how *you* defined love. How does it compare to this agapáō love that Jesus tells us to do? Is it fair to say that maybe we have been thinking about love all wrong? Do you remember in my introduction when I said that from childhood, I had a twisted view of love? By God's grace, we can change this about ourselves.

Paul said in Romans 12:2, *"And do not be conformed to this world, but be transformed by the renewing of your mind, so that you may prove what the will of God is, that which is good and acceptable and perfect."* Over the next few days, we will learn how to be transformed by the renewing of our minds. We are doing this to change our hearts to learn to want what God wants — to love people.

Now that we have defined love, we understand that God is love; love is choosing what God prefers, embracing what God embraces by knowing Him, and unselfishly seeking what's best for others. But what does Godly love look like in action?

Paul's best definition of love is found in 1 Corinthians 10. I suggest you read the whole chapter. I am going to focus on 1 Corinthians 10:4-8: *"Love is patient, love is kind and is not jealous; love does not brag and is not arrogant, does not act unbecomingly; it does not seek its own, is not provoked, does not take into account a wrong suffered, does not rejoice in unrighteousness, but rejoices with the truth; bears all things, believes all things, hopes all things, endures all things. Love never fails."*

For simplicity, I will call these the attributes of Godly love. As I was trying to learn to start showing love to others, I would think about how I treated people and compare my actions to these attributes. It would help me take an inventory of how I was doing.

In Romans 13:8-10, Paul shows us why it is important for us to love: *"Owe nothing to anyone except to love one another; for he who loves his neighbor has fulfilled the law. For this, 'YOU SHALL NOT COMMIT ADULTERY, YOU SHALL NOT MURDER, YOU SHALL NOT STEAL, YOU SHALL NOT COVET,' and if there is any other commandment, it is summed up in this saying, 'YOU SHALL LOVE YOUR NEIGHBOR AS YOURSELF.' Love does no wrong to a neighbor; therefore, love is the fulfillment of the law."* In these verses, Paul explains that love is never meant to purposefully cause harm. If we love our neighbor, we will not want to do them wrong. We have to be careful here, however. Doing our neighbor wrong cannot be based on our understanding but only on God's Word.

For example, let's say I have neighbors who are living in a homosexual relationship with each other. I invite them over to eat dinner with my family. We have a casual conversation to get to know each other during dinner. After dinner, they ask me, "Do you think we are living a sinful lifestyle?" As a follower of Jesus, I must tell them the truth about what the Bible says. As long as I am telling them this truth lovingly and respectfully, being careful to tell them about God's grace and what Jesus did for them, I am not doing them wrong.

They may perceive this coming from me as being hurtful. But this feeling is coming from their perception. They don't believe what God says is true. They are choosing this lifestyle despite how God says to live. Let's look at how the Bible perceives this circumstance. Proverbs 12:17 says, *"He who speaks truth tells what is right, But a false witness, deceit."* Solomon says here that if I were to tell them anything but the truth, I would be deceiving them.

Read 1 Corinthians chapter 8. In this chapter, Paul talks

about being careful not to cause someone else to fall from their faith. In verse 13, he said, *"Therefore, if food causes my brother to stumble, I will never eat meat again, so that I will not cause my brother to stumble."* The word *stumble* is *skandalízō*. It means "to hinder right conduct or thought." [3] In context, Paul said he didn't want to cause anyone to sin. If we affirm behavior that God calls sin, we are taking from them the opportunity to be convicted by the Holy Spirit, leading them into salvation. Is that a loving act, to keep a person from eternal life by lying to them to spare their feelings? I have been guilty of doing this in the past. I was wrong for it.

The Bible is full of love because it is the story of Jesus. I couldn't even begin to touch on the subject in one day. Before we can learn to truly love, we have to allow Jesus, through the power of the Holy Spirit, to transform our hearts. Our hearts are corrupted by sin. We have to remove that sin so that we can replace it with God's love. Then and only then can we truly start loving others the way God wants us to. Tomorrow, we will start learning how to circumcise our hearts by answering the question, "How do I renew my mind?"

> *Before proceeding to the next section, review and ask yourself the self-reflection questions listed in the "How to Use This Devotional" section at the beginning of this book.*

# Day 14 Prayer

Father God, You are worthy, You are worthy of my praise. Father, You have loved me from the day I was born. You have never given up on me; for that, Father, I praise You. You created love so that You could love me and I could love You. Thank you, O' Lord, for loving the world by sending Your Son, Jesus, to allow us to come into Your presence. You are Mighty Lord, awesome in Power, full of grace and truth. Today, You have helped me to see how You view love, Father. I have fallen short of loving others. I have fallen short on loving You as well. Show me, Father, how to love like You love. Teach me to love Your wisdom and truth more. Teach me, Father, through Your Holy Spirit, how to love others. I submit to You all my selfish ways so that I can seek to do what's best for others first in my heart. Teach me, Father, to hate evil and be bold enough to tell the truth in love to others who are doing evil in Your eyes. Help me to lead them back to You. Forgive me, Father, for deceiving others by telling them lies to spare their feelings. That is wrong, and I don't want to sin against You anymore. Help me to love You, Father, with all my heart, all my soul, all my mind, all my strength, and to love my neighbor as myself. I ask all these things in Jesus' Mighty Name, Amen!

# Day 14 Bible Study Questions

Read John chapter 14 and answer the following questions:

1.  In verses 1 through 4, where do you think Jesus is saying He is going?
2.  When Thomas told Jesus that they didn't know the way to where He was going, how did Jesus answer him?
3.  What do you think Jesus means in verse 7 when He says, "If you know Me, you know the Father?"
4.  What are the two reasons Jesus says to believe that He is in the Father and the Father is in Him?
    a.  What do you think this says about God's nature toward mankind?
5.  Who will Jesus send to be with us when He leaves to be with the Father in Heaven?
6.  How does Jesus tell us to love Him?
7.  What does Jesus say that He will do for us if we show the love to Him that He asks?
8.  What is the role of the Helper Jesus sends to us while He is gone?
9.  What is the last thing Jesus says He will give us after He is gone?

# Day 15: How do I Renew My Mind?

Why is it important for us to renew our minds? Paul speaks of this in Romans 12:1-2. He says, *"Therefore I urge you, brethren, by the mercies of God, to present your bodies a living and holy sacrifice, acceptable to God, which is your spiritual service of worship. And do not be conformed to this world, but be transformed by the renewing of your mind, so that you may prove what the will of God is, that which is good and acceptable and perfect."*

In verse one, Paul tells us how to worship God spiritually. We must present ourselves as a living and holy sacrifice, acceptable to God. What is the sacrifice we have to make? We have to stop living our lives to please ourselves and start living our lives to please God. The word *holy* means "set apart." God wants us to set ourselves apart to fully worship Him.

How do I know if I am living my life to please myself or to please God? This is where self-examination comes in. Think about the conversations and thoughts you have throughout the day. What are they centered on? Are they centered on yourself or on God? How much time do you give God every day? The answers to these questions show why we need to renew our hearts and minds.

Paul continues his thought in Romans 12:3: *"For through the grace given to me I say to everyone among you not to think more highly of himself than he ought to think; but to think so as to have sound judgment, as God has allotted to each a measure of faith."* Let's analyze this verse in more detail to uncover the true meaning in the original language.

The word used for *highly* is *hyperphronéō*. It means "to think beyond which exceeds proper (appropriate) limits or to act high-minded because a lack of humility as well as a true sense of reality." [1] What is the reality here in God's eyes? We are all equally important to God. He loves each and every one of us the same way. We have missed the mark if we think we deserve more than another person for any reason.

Next, in Romans 12:2, Paul says we need *"to be transformed by the renewing of our mind."* What does the word *transformed* really mean? The word for *transformed, metamorphóō*, means "transformed after being with. It is also used of the Lord transforming (changing) believers as they walk in faith." [2] The Lord is changing us as we walk in faith.

What is faith? The word used for *faith* is *pístis* which means "persuaded. In its biblical sense, faith is always received by believers." [3] What Paul said in Romans 12:3 aligns with this definition. He said, *"as God has allotted to each a measure of faith."* God gives each of us, when we are saved, the faith we need to carry out His will. What God doesn't do is force us to obey. We have to choose to submit ourselves to His will. This is another reason we have to transform our minds. We must allow God to persuade us that His will is best for us.

Let's summarize what we have learned before we move on. To spiritually worship God, we have to humbly present ourselves before Him as holy. When we do that, we trust God through faith, his in-birthed persuasion, to help us view ourselves rightly, through sound judgment, as equal to everyone in this world that God has created. Once we see ourselves and others as God sees us, we can start to properly love as He wants us to love.

Listen to what Paul said in Ephesus in Ephesians 4:17-19: *"So this I say, and affirm together with the Lord, that you walk no longer just as the Gentiles also walk, in the futility of their mind, being darkened in their understanding, excluded from the life of God because of the ignorance that is in them, because of the hardness of their heart; and they, having become callous, have given themselves over to sensuality for the practice of every kind of impurity with greediness."*

Paul is pleading to the believers in Ephesus to live changed lives. He describes how the Gentiles, a term used to describe the Greeks at the time, were living sinful, ungodly lives because they refused to believe the truth about Jesus. I am calling for you to examine yourself to determine if you are living in ignorance of any idolatry or sin in your life so that you can overcome it.

Paul continues his appeal in Ephesians 4:20-23: *"But you did not learn Christ in this way, if indeed you have heard Him and have been taught in Him, just as truth is in Jesus, that, in reference to your former manner of life, you lay aside the old self, which is being corrupted in accordance with the lusts of deceit, and that you be renewed in the spirit of your mind, and put on the new self, which in the likeness of God has been created in righteousness and holiness of the truth."*

Paul is making the same appeal to the church in Ephesus that He did for the church in Rome — to renew their mind. Look how Paul describes the old self here. He says, *"which is being corrupted in accordance with the lusts of deceit."* The word for *lusts* is *epithymía*. It means "passionate desire built on a particular feeling (urge) which can be positive or negative — depending on whether such is inspired by faith. Epithymía usually refers to yearnings that grow out of the desires of self. However, it is not evil in and of itself. It only becomes bad when the strong feelings build on what misses God's mark." [4]

Paul said the old self is being corrupted by the lusts of deceit. In other words, before you were a follower of Jesus, you were being deceived. Now that you have been made aware of your sin, it's time to put off that deception and walk in truth. Paul says we should *"be renewed in the spirit of our minds, and put on the new self, which in the likeness of God has been created in righteousness and holiness of the truth."*

This is a big statement. He wants us to be renewed in our minds and put on the new self. Why? We have been born again in the spirit, which, in the likeness of God, has been created in righteousness and holiness of the truth. Think about that. Paul is saying that once we are born again, we wear righteousness and holiness of truth. This doesn't come from us but from the blood that Jesus shed that covers the filthiness of our sin. How amazing is that?

Paul continues in Ephesians 4:25-32: *"Therefore, laying aside falsehood, SPEAK TRUTH EACH ONE of you WITH HIS NEIGHBOR, for we are members of one another. BE ANGRY, AND yet DO NOT SIN; do not let the sun go down on your anger, and do not give the devil an opportunity. He who steals must steal no longer; but rather he must labor, performing with his own hands what is good, so that he will have something to share with one who has need. Let no unwholesome word proceed from your mouth, but only such a word as is good for edification according to the need of the moment, so that it will give grace to those who hear. Do not grieve the Holy Spirit of God, by whom you were sealed for the day of redemption. Let all bitterness and wrath and anger and clamor and slander be put away from you, along with all malice. Be kind to one another, tender-hearted, forgiving each other, just as God in Christ also has forgiven you."*

Paul said in Colossians 3:5-11: *"Therefore consider the members of your earthly body as dead to immorality, impurity, passion, evil desire, and greed, which amounts to idolatry. For it is because of these things that the wrath of God will come upon the sons of disobedience, and in them you also once walked, when you were living in them. But know you also, put them all aside: anger, wrath, malice, slander, and abusive speech from your mouth. Do not lie to one another, since you laid aside the old self with its evil practices, and have put on the new self who is being renewed to a true knowledge according to the image of the One who created him — a renewal in which there is no distinction between Greek and Jew, circumcised and uncircumcised, barbarian, Scythian, slave and freeman, but Christ is all, and in all."*

These are the things Paul says for us to put off. We must evaluate our lives to see if we are doing any of these things. If we find ourselves doing any of these things, we need to evaluate our hearts and ask ourselves why. How are these behaviors meeting our needs that we keep on doing them? How can we transform our hearts and minds to allow God to meet our needs in a healthier way besides causing another person harm? God wants us to learn to rely on His love to fill our hearts. When we do that, we are fully equipped to go out into the world and love one another just as God loves us. The question for tomorrow will be, "What do I put on?"

*Before proceeding to the next section, review and ask yourself the self-reflection questions listed in the "How to Use This Devotional" section at the beginning of this book.*

# Day 15 Prayer

Father God, today I learned that even though I have been saved, my heart is still wicked in Your eyes. Father, You have the power to make the sun rise and set. You placed every star in heaven where it is and sustained them. You tell the wind when to blow and the waves when to crash. You even make the air the perfect concentration of oxygen, nitrogen, and carbon so I can breathe. Father, since You can do all these things and more, I know you can help me put off the wickedness in my heart and mind so that I can glorify You with my life. Father, help me to see Your creation the way You see it. Help me to see people the way You see them. Help me to love others before I love myself. Most of all, Father, help me learn to rely on You and You alone to provide me all the love I need. When You do this, Father, I will be able to receive whatever love others have for me, accept it, and know that it's enough because I know that You love me. Your love is enough, Father. For that, I thank You. Who am I, Father, that you would love me enough to send Your Son Jesus to die for me? I am Your creation, created to do good works to bring You glory. Father, I am ready to submit my heart to You to do those works. Thank You, Father. In Jesus' Mighty Name, I pray, Amen!

# Day 15 Bible Study Questions

Read John chapter 15 and answer the following questions:

1. What do you think Jesus means by pruning His branches?
2. How does Jesus say we can bear fruit?
3. How does Jesus say His Father is glorified?
4. What commandment does Jesus give?
5. Why does Jesus say the world would hate His followers?
6. What does Jesus do about it in verse 19?
7. Did Jesus do anything to deserve their hate?
8. What does Jesus say the Helper would do?

# Day 16: What Do I Put On?

What have we learned so far about our hearts? We have recognized that our hearts and our minds are sinful. We have searched our hearts to expose any evil thoughts. We have been given examples of those evil thoughts to help us know what to look for. As we begin putting off our evil ways, what do we put on instead?

Following Jesus is not only about what we cannot do. If it were, that would mean God is oppressive and cruel. That is not who God is. How do I know this to be true? Jesus Himself made this claim about God. Mark 10:18 says, *"And Jesus said to him, 'Why do you call Me good? No one is good except God alone.'"*

Psalms 84:11 says, *"For the Lord God is a sun and shield; The Lord gives grace and glory; No good thing does He withhold from those who walk uprightly."* Jesus said God the Father Himself is good. And the Psalmist said that God doesn't withhold anything good for those who walk uprightly. This poses the question, "What does God say is good for us to do?" These things are what we should start doing.

Paul says in Philippians 4:4-8, *"Rejoice in the Lord always; again, I will say, rejoice! Let your gentle spirit be known to all men. The Lord is near. Be anxious for nothing, but in everything by prayer and supplication with thanksgiving let your requests be made known to God. And the peace of God, which surpasses all comprehension, will guard your hearts and your minds in Christ*

*Jesus.*

*"Finally, brethren, whatever is true, whatever is honorable, whatever is right, whatever is pure, whatever is lovely, whatever is of good repute, if there is any excellence and if anything, worthy of praise, dwell on these things."*

First, we need to start recognizing God for who He is. He is our God the Creator; Elohim, the Most High God; El Elyon, our Banner or our protector and defender; Yahweh Nissi, our Provider; Yahweh Yireh, our Healer; Jehovah Rapha, God Almighty; El Shaddai, the God who sees us; El Roi, the great I AM; Yahweh, and God our Father, Abba.

For these reasons, we need to always rejoice in Him. Because of who He is, we do not have to be afraid. Rather, we can let Him know our needs, wait on Him to provide what He knows is best for us, and thank Him for it. When we do this, He will give peace far beyond anything we could ever imagine.

When we put Him in the proper place in our hearts, we will start to see ourselves the way He sees us. We are participants in building His Kingdom with Him. We are equal to every other believer in the world. This gives us the proper humility to renew our minds in Christ Jesus.

Paul then says we need to focus our thoughts on what is true, honorable, right, pure, lovely, of good repute, and anything excellent or worthy of praise. These things will help bring joy to our hearts and minds when we learn to focus on good rather than evil. But that is only the beginning.

Paul said in Colossians 3:1-4, *"Therefore if you have been raised up with Christ, keep seeking the things above, where Christ is, seated at the right hand of God. Set your mind on the things above, not on the things that are on earth. For you have died and your life is hidden with Christ in God. When Christ, who is our life, is revealed, then you also will be revealed with Him in glory."*

Paul says we must ask ourselves, "What does God say

about that?" All the pressure comes off us when we focus on how God says we should do something instead of relying on ourselves to make that decision. This way, we learn how to think about things differently than we did before. This renews our minds and starts to heal our hearts.

Paul also says our lives have been hidden with Christ in God. This means we are not inhabitants of this world anymore but citizens of Heaven with God. When Jesus returns, we will return with Him in glory. Isn't that amazing?

Paul continued in Colossians 3:12-17, "*So, as those who have been chosen of God, holy and beloved, put on a heart of compassion, kindness, humility, gentleness and patience; bearing with one another, and forgiving each other, whoever has a complaint against anyone; just as the Lord forgave you, so also should you. Beyond all these things put on love, which is the perfect bond of unity. Let the peace of Christ rule in your hearts, to which indeed you were called in one body; and be thankful. Let the word of Christ richly dwell within you, with all wisdom teaching and admonishing one another with psalms and hymns and spiritual songs, singing with thankfulness in your hearts to God. Whatever you do in word or deed, do all in the name of the Lord Jesus, giving thanks through Him to God the Father.*"

If every person you met treated you as Paul mentioned above, would your life be easier than it is? If you started treating people like Paul mentioned above, do you think people would react to you differently? If so, how do you think it would be different? This is what God views as good. This is how God wants us to live our lives.

In Romans 12:9-18, Paul says, "*Let love be without hypocrisy. Abhor what is evil; cling to what is good. Be devoted to one another in brotherly love; give preference to one another in honor; not lagging behind in diligence, fervent in spirit, serving the Lord; rejoicing in hope, persevering in tribulation, devoted to prayer, contributing to the needs of the saints, practicing hospitality.*

*"Bless those who persecute you; bless and do not curse. Rejoice with those who rejoice, and weep with those who weep. Be of the same mind toward one another; do not be haughty in mind, but associate with the lowly. Do not be wise in your own estimation. Never pay back evil for evil to anyone. Respect what is right in the sight of all men. If possible, so far as it depends on you, be at peace with all men."*

Finally, Paul says in Galatians 5:16-25 how we should live our lives: *"But I say, walk by the Spirit, and you will not carry out the desire of the flesh. For the flesh sets its desire against the Spirit, and the Spirit against the flesh; for these are in opposition to one another, so that you may not do the things that you please. But if you are led by the Spirit, you are not under the Law. Now the deeds of the flesh are evident, which are: immorality, impurity, sensuality, idolatry, sorcery, enmities, strife, jealousy, outbursts of anger, disputes, dissensions, factions, envying, drunkenness, carousing, and things like these, of which I forewarn you, just as I have forewarned you, that those who practice such things will not inherit the kingdom of God. But the fruit of the Spirit is love, joy, peace, patience, kindness, goodness, faithfulness, gentleness, self-control; against such things there is no law. Now those who belong to Christ Jesus have crucified the flesh with its passions and desires. If we live by the Spirit, let us also walk by the Spirit."*

Paul describes how to live by the spirit and not by the flesh. I will be honest. In the beginning, as you are making these changes, they will not be easy. We must rely on the power of the Holy Spirit in us as we seek God to help us. We cannot do it on our own.

This is another reason I say to find someone to go through this journey with you. You can help hold each other accountable to learn how to live by the spirit and not by the flesh. You have to be completely honest with one another. This is not meant for judgment but rather to encourage one another to learn how to live for Christ. Tomorrow, we will answer the question, "How do I help others bear spiritual fruit?"

> *Before proceeding to the next section, review and ask yourself the self-reflection questions listed in the "How to Use This Devotional" section at the beginning of this book.*

# Day 16 Prayer

Father God, as I search my heart for the sin I need to remove, help me learn how to put on the truth instead. Father, Your Son Jesus is the truth. Help me to know You deeper, Father, to learn about Your attributes and character and how You see me as I am now. Help me to know what to take off and what to put on. Father, help me think about what You say is good, true, honorable, right, pure, lovely, of good repute, excellent, and praiseworthy. I want to learn to dwell on these things instead of worldly thoughts, my selfish lusts, and desires. I submit these evil thoughts to You, Father. Help me to always remember that I have been made new and my life is hidden with You in Heaven. Help me be thankful, Father, for who You are and that You would even think of me. Help me to put on a heart of compassion, kindness, humility, gentleness, and patience. Help me be honest with not only myself but the person with whom I am reading this devotional so that I can be accountable to myself, You, and another person. I can't do this alone, Father; I put my trust in You and You alone. I pray these things to You in Jesus' Mighty Name, Amen!

# Day 16 Bible Study Questions

Read John chapter 16 and answer the following questions:

1. In verses 1 through 4, what is Jesus warning His disciples about?
2. What did Jesus say the advantage would be for Him going away?
3. What three things will the Helper convict of?
4. What did Jesus say the second role of the Helper would be?
5. What do you think Jesus meant in verse 16?
6. How does Jesus say we should ask of the Father?
7. Where does Jesus say He is going?
8. In verse 33, why does Jesus say we should have courage?

# Day 17: How Do I Help Others Bear Spiritual Fruit?

In Galatians 5:16, Paul says, *"But I say, walk by the Spirit, and you will not carry out the desire of the flesh."* It is important for us to search our hearts to recognize if we are walking in the Spirit. How do we know if we are walking in the Spirit? Paul tells us.

In Galatians 5:22, Paul says, *"But the fruit of the Spirit is love, joy, peace, patience, kindness, goodness, faithfulness, gentleness, self-control; against such things there is no law."* As we search our hearts, evidence of the fruit of the Spirit will give us a sign of how we are doing. If we see this change in ourselves, then we are doing good. If we do not, we must search our hearts and ask ourselves why. Some questions we may ask ourselves are as follows:

1. Are there any struggles I am facing keeping me from producing spiritual fruit?
2. What choices am I making that are causing problems in my life, preventing me from producing spiritual fruit?
    a. What does God say about these choices?
    b. If God calls these choices sin, what should I do about it?
3. Is there someone in my life that I feel is treating me unfairly?

     a. How does God say in the Bible that I should
       deal with that person?

4. Do I have an area of idolatry in my life that I have not admitted to?

5. Do I have an area of my life that I haven't submitted to God?

6. Am I spending time reading the Bible and praying every day?

7. Have I recently stopped seeking God altogether?

Before I can help anyone else bear fruit, I have to ensure my heart is circumcised and that I am bearing fruit. If I do not do this first, I will be giving people advice from my understanding and not God's.

Jesus speaks about this topic in Matthew 7:1-5. He says, *""Do not judge so that you will not be judged. For in the way you judge, you will be judged; and by your standard of measure, it will be measured to you. Why do you look at the speck that is in your brother's eye, but do not notice the log that is in your own eye? Or how can you say to your brother, 'Let me take the speck out of your eye, and behold, the log is in your own eye?' You hypocrite, first take the log out of your own eye, and then you will see clearly to take the speck out of your brother's eye."*

Matthew 7:1 is one of the many misinterpreted quotes in the Bible. Jesus is not telling people not to judge at all. That would be a lie. Jesus can't lie because He is the truth. We all have to make judgments all the time. Jesus is talking about people who are judging hypocritically. That means they are pointing their finger at someone who is doing something they are doing as well.

Jesus says before we can properly help someone overcome a sin, we must search our hearts to ensure we aren't sinning in the same way. That is why Jesus told them to take the log out of their own eye before trying to take the speck out of someone else's eye. I have spent over four years learning how to put away my idolatry so that I could write this book to help you do the same.

In Luke chapter 13, some people came to Jesus, asking Him a hypocritical question. Jesus knew they were trying to judge others for sin when they had unresolved sin in their hearts. Look at what He said in Luke 13: *"'I tell you, no, but unless you repent, you will all likewise perish.' And He began telling this parable: 'A man had a fig tree which had been planted in his vineyard; and he came looking for fruit on it and did not find any. And he said to the vineyard-keeper, 'Behold, for three years I have come looking for fruit on this fig tree without finding any. Cut it down! Why does it even use up the ground?' And he answered and said to him, 'Let it alone, sir, for this year too, until I dig around it and put in fertilizer; and if it bears fruit next year, fine; but if not, cut it down.'"*

In this parable, Jesus is talking about two people. The first person is the man who owns the vineyard. The second person is the vinedresser who works for the owner. The fig tree represents something that belongs to the owner of the vineyard. The owner is God, the vinedresser is Jesus, and the fig tree represents someone who is a part of God's creation but isn't bearing any spiritual fruit. This person isn't doing anything useful for the Kingdom of God.

Jesus, the vinedresser in this parable, advocates for the person represented by the fig tree. Jesus asks the Father to give Him more time to work on his heart so that maybe he will start producing spiritual fruit. But when the time has come for the harvest, if he has not produced fruit, then he will be destroyed. Jesus is giving an example of how we should consider those around us needing to be saved. We should do all we can to help them come to Jesus and be effective in the Kingdom like Jesus did.

Look at another parable Jesus gives in John 15:1-6, *"I am*

*the true vine, and My Father is the vinedresser. "Every branch in Me that does not bear fruit, He takes away; and every branch that bears fruit, He prunes it so that it may bear more fruit. "You are already clean because of the word which I have spoken to you. "Abide in Me, and I in you. As the branch cannot bear fruit of itself unless it abides in the vine, so neither can you unless you abide in Me. "I am the vine, you are the branches; he who abides in Me and I in him, he bears much fruit, for apart from Me you can do nothing. "If anyone does not abide in Me, he is thrown away as a branch and dries up; and they gather them, and cast them into the fire and they are burned."*

What does the word *fruit* really mean? The word for *fruit* is *karpós*. Figuratively, it means "everything done in true partnership with Christ. Fruit in the Bible is only produced when decisions are inspired and empowered by the Lord. Fruitful deeds can only happen by obeying God through faith." [1]

Jesus later said in John 15:16-17, *"You did not choose Me but I chose you, and appointed you that you would go and bear fruit, and that your fruit would remain, so that whatever you ask of the Father in My name He may give to you. "This I command you, that you love one another."*

Jesus is saying that not only do we need Him in order to bear fruit, but He chose us and appointed us so that we would go and bear fruit. How do we bear fruit? We abide in Jesus. That means we need to be constantly seeking Jesus daily in the Bible and praying to Him to help us grow closer to Him so that we can bear spiritual fruit. If we refuse to believe in Jesus before our time is up, we will be sent to Hell. There is a sense of urgency here because I don't know about you, but I don't want anyone to suffer eternally in hell.

How do we help others bear spiritual fruit? The first thing we have to do is make sure they know Jesus. He is the only way they can bear fruit. Once they have been spiritually reborn through belief in Him, we are called to have a relationship with them, encouraging them to remain in Him and receiving encouragement from them. This process is called discipleship.

After Jesus was raised from the dead in His glorified body before He ascended to heaven, He revealed Himself to His disciples and others. After He was risen, Jesus gave the only command from His authority. It's called the Great Commission. Matthew 28:18-20 says, *"And Jesus came up and spoke to them, saying, "All authority has been given to Me in heaven and on earth. "Go therefore and make disciples of all the nations, baptizing them in the name of the Father and the Son and the Holy Spirit, teaching them to observe all that I commanded you; and lo, I am with you always, even to the end of the age."*

The process of discipleship is how Jesus wants us to teach each other people about who He is, how to follow Him, and how to bear spiritual fruit for the Kingdom of Heaven. This is what Jesus wants us to do for the rest of our lives while we are waiting for Him to return. Tomorrow, we answer the question, "What is a disciple?"

> *Before proceeding to the next section, review and ask yourself the self-reflection questions listed in the "How to Use This Devotional" section at the beginning of this book.*

# Day 17 Prayer

Father God, today, I learned that to help others bear spiritual fruit, I must learn how to do it myself. I need Jesus to help me with that, Father. He is the only way I can bear fruit. "Create in me a clean heart, O God, and renew a steadfast spirit within me. Do not cast me away from Your presence, and do not take Your Holy Spirit from me. Restore to me the joy of Your salvation, and sustain me with a willing spirit. Then I will teach transgressors Your ways, and sinners will be converted to You. Deliver me from blood guiltiness, O God, the God of my salvation; Then my tongue will joyfully sing of Your righteousness. O Lord, open my lips, that my mouth may declare You praise. For You do not delight in sacrifice, otherwise I would give it; You are not pleased with burnt offering. The sacrifices of God are a broken spirit; A broken and a contrite heart, O God, You will not despise" [2]. Father, once You have prepared my heart to serve You, lead me to those around me who don't know you. Give me the words to say, Your words, that I may bring them out of the darkness into Your wondrous light. Help me to encourage those who know You and send people into my life to encourage me. I pray these things in Jesus' Mighty Name, Amen!

# Day 17 Bible Study Questions

Read John chapter 17 and answer the following questions:

1.  In His prayer, what does Jesus say is eternal life?
2.  When did Jesus say He had glory?
3.  What did Jesus tell His Father that He was doing for His disciples while He was with them?
4.  Why did Jesus say that the world hated His disciples?
5.  What did Jesus ask His Father to sanctify His disciples in?
6.  In verse 20, who do you think Jesus is saying He is praying for other than His disciples?
7.  In verse 24, what did Jesus ask His Father to show them?
8.  How long did Jesus say His Father had loved Him?
9.  What did Jesus come to make known to the people of the world?

# Day 18: What is a Disciple?

Before I talk about what a disciple is, I will explain why it is important for us to make disciples. Next, I will explain the Great Commission in detail. Then I will define what a disciple, discipler, and disciple-making are. Then I will discuss some of the strategies Jesus used to make disciples.

Proverbs 29:18 says, *"Where there is no vision, the people are unrestrained, but happy is he who keeps the law."* The Hebrew word for *vision* used here is *ḥāzôn*. It means "divine revelation." [1] What have we been talking about learning how to do? To want what God wants. We need His vision.

What does God really want? The answer is people. 1 Timothy 2:3-4 says, *"This is good and acceptable in the sight of God our Savior, who desires all men to be saved and to come to the knowledge of the truth."* This is the reason why disciple-making is so important. God wants to use us to help multiply His Kingdom by bringing others to faith in Jesus.

The word for *unrestrained* is *para* which simply means "to let alone." [2] In John 3:20, Jesus tells of the judgment that people are already in. It says, *"For everyone who does evil hates the Light, and does not come to the Light for fear that his deeds will be exposed."* They want to be left alone.

What happens to them if we leave them alone? They will perish because they didn't believe in Jesus. This perishing isn't just physical death; it's the eternal separation from God we discussed on day six. God doesn't want anyone to die and go to Hell. He wants us to do our best to help them learn about Jesus so they can be saved. That's why disciple-making is so important.

In Matthew 28:18-20, Jesus says, *"All authority has been given to Me in heaven and on earth. Go therefore and make disciples of all the nations, baptizing them in the name of the Father and the Son and the Holy Spirit, teaching them to observe all that I commanded you; and lo, I am with you always, even to the end of the age."*

As far as I know, this is the first command that Jesus gave His disciples under the authority that God gave Him after His resurrection. That means it's important to Jesus. If it's important to Jesus and we are His followers, then it should also be important to us.

Jesus says He has all the authority in heaven and on earth. We are now all under His jurisdiction. He says, "Because I have this authority and I taught you how to follow Me, now you go out and teach others how to follow Me." The only command given in the great commission is to make disciples. The word in Greek that is used for *go* is *poreúomai.* It means "as you are going." [3] The word for *make disciples* is *mathēteúō.* It means "to help someone to progressively learn the Word of God to become a matured disciple." [4]

This command to make disciples was a mandate to each individual believer because Jesus told this to His disciples before they established the church. Jesus expects every believer to develop a mentor-teacher relationship with an older and a younger believer to help them best grasp the truths of the Word of God.

The last part of the Great Commission is Jesus giving us His encouragement. He is saying He will be with us as we are discipling others, helping us along the way for eternity. This not only draws us into closer relationships with other believers but also with Jesus because we need Him to do it effectively.

A *disciple* of Jesus is a committed, lifelong learner and follower of Jesus. This commitment is not only to learn about Jesus but also to help other believers grow in their spiritual maturity. A *discipler* teaches a less mature believer, helping them grow in knowledge and faith into a more mature believer. A *disciple-maker* helps other people learn how to make disciples themselves.

The first step in disciple-making is to go out into the world to find someone willing to learn more about Jesus with you. They need a teachable spirit, which means a willingness to learn. This could be someone who already believes or a person who doesn't believe but who is willing to listen.

You can start by being led of the Spirit to walk up to someone and ask them to meet you for lunch or coffee. Take time to get to know them, and when the opportunity arises, tell them about Jesus. Once you have an established relationship, you can start the next phase of disciple-making.

We have to be intentional. We need to study the Bible with them, teaching about Jesus while intentionally teaching them to train others about what they have learned. We should be having regular discussions with them several times a week. We have to spend time together.

We have to always remember that disciple-making is never a one-way street. We have to be willing to listen and learn from each other. God can use others to teach us life lessons as well.

Another important thing in disciple-making is accountability. We first must model the behavior that we want them to learn. And we must be willing to encourage them when needed to make sure they are growing in faith and not stagnant. For this to work effectively, it needs to be one-on-one or in small groups. Disciple-making takes time and dedication.

We need to help others learn to be self-reliant, teaching them to study and learn on their own as well as learning from us. I have grown closer to Jesus while I was seeking Him on my own by reading the Bible. I can't expect to have a personal relationship with someone without meeting them in person. Jesus is the Word. That's where we go to meet Him.

Not only do we encourage them to learn about Jesus with us, but we should also teach them the need to be involved in a local congregation. This can help them grow in faith under a good pastor who is properly teaching the Word of God. The pastor will be another person to help them understand the Bible. It will give them opportunities to serve the Lord in their community. Serving others is a great way to find new people to disciple. As a discipler, it also provides an opportunity to model serving others and teach them how to do the same.

I want to offer some encouragement now. If you desire to help others in discipleship training, don't give up. When God has fully prepared you, He will send you someone to disciple. We must remember we are working on His time-line, not our own.

I highly recommend reading the book *Tally Ho the Fox* by Herb Hodges. It is an awesome resource to help you learn how to be a disciple and teach others disciple-making. It is a very easy book to read and understand. Herb's disciple-making ministry has reached people worldwide through this book.

For the next three days, I want to talk about what happens when we start to find ourselves falling back into our idols, how to start healing from the damage our idols have caused us, and how to move forward in a relationship with Jesus once we are done reading this devotional. I will suggest other books to read that have helped me grow in faith and heal from the damage the idols caused.

*Before proceeding to the next section, review and ask yourself the self-reflection questions listed in the "How to Use This Devotional" section at the beginning of this book.*

# Day 18 Prayer

Father God, today, I learned more about what it really means to be a disciple of Jesus. I learned that in order for me to want what You want, I have to want people. Father, You desire all men to be saved and come to the knowledge of the Truth. Help me to learn how to bring others into the knowledge of the Truth, who I know is Your Son, Jesus. Father, help me to submit myself to the authority that You gave Your Son Jesus when You raised Him from the dead. Help me to obey all the things He taught me to do, part of which is discipling others. Help me love other people the way You do and see other people the way You see them. Give me the vision You have for me so that I do what You want to keep people from perishing. I love you, Father, and Your Son, Jesus. I want to submit myself to You as a holy and living sacrifice, faithful and pleasing to You. Help me to do that. I ask You all these things in Jesus' Mighty Name, Amen!

# Day 18 Bible Study Questions

Read John chapter 18 and answer the following questions:

1. How did Judas Iscariot betray Jesus?
2. When they came to seize Jesus, what did He ask them to do regarding His disciples?
    a. Why did Jesus ask them this?
3. What did Peter do to try to protect Jesus?
    a. How did Jesus rebuke him?
4. How many times did Peter deny Jesus?
    a. What happened immediately after?
5. Who did Caiaphas take Jesus before first?
6. What was Pilate's initial response to Caiaphas?
7. What was the first question Pilate asked Jesus?
8. Why do you think Jesus said His Kingdom wasn't of this world?
    a. Where do you think Jesus' Kingdom was?
9. What did Jesus come to testify of?
10. What did Pilate ask next?
    a. Why is this question important?
11. Who did the Jews want to be released instead of Jesus?

# Day 19: What if I Fall Back Into Temptation?

Some people want to make it seem as if once you become a follower of Jesus, you have everything figured out. That isn't really true. Every honest believer knows that without Jesus, we can't do anything right. Remember what Jesus said in John 15:5, *"apart from Me you can do nothing."* Salvation is the beginning of Christianity, not the end.

What happens if I stop playing video games, start seeking Jesus, and become saved, but after a while, I find myself being drawn back into video games? That's a good question, and I would like to explain some things.

First, because we have made something an idol to us in the past doesn't necessarily mean that doing it is a sin. Using social media or playing video games aren't sins in God's eyes. Those are just things we do. The problem is when we put those things ahead of seeking a relationship with Jesus.

Paul said in 2 Corinthians 4:16, *"Therefore we do not lose heart, but though our outer man is decaying, yet our inner man is being renewed day by day."* Our salvation doesn't come from our works. Paul later said in Ephesians 2:8-9, *"For by grace you have been saved through faith; and that not of yourselves, it is the gift of God; not as a result of works, so that no one may boast."* If we could be good enough on our own to be saved, we wouldn't have needed Jesus in the first place. This takes all of the pressure off us and puts it on the only one who can handle it, Jesus. Jesus is renewing us every day.

Paul said something similar in Colossians 3:9-10: *"Do not lie to one another, since you laid aside the old self with its evil practices, and have put on the new self who is being renewed to a true knowledge according to the image of the One who created him."* Let's look at the deeper meaning of 2 Corinthians 4:16 and Colossians 3:9-10.

The word used in both verses for *renew* is *anakainóō*. It literally means "to renew by completing a process." [1] Which process is Paul speaking of? The process is called sanctification. Paul says in 1 Thessalonians 4:3, *"For this is the will of God, your sanctification."* Let's look deeper into the meaning of sanctification.

The word used for *sanctification* is *hagiasmós*. This word is derived from *hágios*, which means *holy*. It means "the process of advancing holiness. Sanctification is used of the believer progressively transformed by the Lord into His likeness. It emphasizes how God alone initiates and accomplishes holiness, in the person wanting his "differentness" to be set apart as special." [2]

Let's go back and look at *anakainóō*, the word used for *renew*. This refers to "the powerful work of Christ which renews (transforms) the willing heart. Both times referring to God ever-transforming the believer by renewing 'the new man' in Christ." [1] The words for *renew* and *sanctification* show that God's the one doing the work in us; we just have to have a willing heart to be changed.

Now we understand that we have to cling to our new identity in Christ to be changed and that sanctification is the process by which God makes us new when we submit our hearts to Him. Let's revisit our question. What do I do when I fail to do what I am supposed to do?

First, we must remember that we aren't perfect but are being perfected each day by God's work in us through faith. That means we will make mistakes. But if we are honest with ourselves and God, we repent by praying to God, apologize for failing, and ask Him to help us succeed. Then stop doing what we shouldn't be doing and start doing what we should be doing again. This is a continuous process we will be doing for the rest of our lives. That's what sanctification means.

Philippians 1:6 says, *"For I am confident of this very thing, that He who began a good work in you will perfect it until the day of Christ Jesus."* This is where our hope comes from. When we commit our hearts to Jesus, He will finish the work He started in us, eventually perfecting us when we are united with Him after death or on the day of His return.

Look at what Jesus said to His disciples in Luke 17:3-4: *"Be on your guard! If your brother sins, rebuke him; and if he repents, forgive him. And if he sins against you seven times a day, and returns to you seven times, saying, 'I repent, ' forgive him."* This is why we need to disciple one another. Jesus first says, "Be on your guard!" The word for *guard* used here is *proséxō*, which means "stay on course; setting a course and keeping to it." [3] Another word to describe it would be *vigilance*.

Next, Jesus says to watch out for each other. When a brother sins, let him know. And when he comes back to repent, forgive him. Jesus says to forgive him seven times a day if he sins against you. If Jesus tells us to do that for each other, how much more would He do that for us?

I would suggest starting every day with reading the Bible. Proverbs 7:1-3 says, *"My son, keep my words, and treasure my commandments within you. Keep my commandments and live, and my teaching as the apple of your eye. Bind them on your fingers; write them on the tablet of your heart."* When you read the Bible, it gets your mind where it is supposed to be, on things above, as Paul said. It also fills you with the Holy Spirit so that you can resist the temptation of the devil. When we have the Word of God written on our hearts, it is harder for us to be deceived.

Mark 6:7 says, *"And He summoned the twelve and began to send them out in pairs, and gave them authority over the unclean spirits..."* When Jesus sent out His disciples to practice what He had taught them, He sent them out in pairs. Jesus never meant for us to be alone in our walk of faith. He wants us to help each other.

If you find yourself struggling to avoid the temptation of returning to your idols, first remember what Paul says in 1 Corinthians 10:13: *"No temptation has overtaken you but such as is common to man; and God is faithful, who will not allow you to be tempted beyond what you are able, but with the temptation will provide the way of escape also, so that you will be able to endure it."* The focus is always on God. It says God is faithful, and He will not allow you to be tempted beyond what you are able. With the temptation, He provided the way out. Remember, the key to overcoming Your idols is Jesus. He is the way out.

First, stop what you are doing and start seeking Jesus in the Word. Then ask for help. There are many resources available. Many churches now have Christian-based recovery groups like *Celebrate Recovery*. Celebrate Recovery is a national organization that churches use to help their members recover from hurts, habits, or hang-ups. You can find more information about it at www.celebraterecovery.com. This is just one of the many organizations that can help.

Another thing you can do is to talk to your pastor about your struggles. He is there to help. Also, I have created a Facebook Page for this book at https://fb.me/findingjesus-book. Feel free to message me if you need help. The page will be a community where believers can connect with each other to find the support they need to learn to walk with Jesus.

You can also look up Christian counselors in your area.

They have been trained to help you walk obediently in your faith with Jesus. They are familiar with what you are going through and can lead you in the right direction.

If the temptation to return to your idol(s) is too strong for you to resist, I would suggest removing it completely from your life. Remember what Jesus said about cutting off your hand if it causes you to sin. [4] He didn't mean that literally, but figuratively. Remove yourself from the source of temptation.

Tomorrow, we are going to discuss the topic of boundaries. Boundaries are an important tool to put in place to help us stay on track. The question I am asking is, "Why can't I have a beer after work?"

*Before proceeding to the next section, review and ask yourself the self-reflection questions listed in the "How to Use This Devotional" section at the beginning of this book.*

# Day 19 Prayer

Father God, today, I learned that sometimes I will fail. But I am putting my trust in You to keep me because Your Word says that He who started a good work in me will perfect it until the return of Christ Jesus. I believe you, God. Help me find people to help me work out my faith so that when I am struggling, I will have someone to help me. And use me to help others who are struggling because I want what You want, Father, and you want people. Help me have the strength to continually read Your Word, Father, because when I write Your Words on the tablet of my heart, they will always be with me. Give me Your strength to resist the temptation of the enemy. Father, I believe You when You say that You will not allow me to be tempted beyond what I can bear. You already gave me the way out through Your Son Jesus; thank you for that, Father. Give me the courage to seek help when I feel weak or struggling. And if I need to, Father, remove all my desires for my idols so I can completely cut them out of my life. I would rather lose my idol than lose You, Father, for eternity. I love you, Father. I pray these things to you in Jesus' Mighty Name, Amen!

# Day 19 Bible Study Questions

Read John chapter 19 and answer the following questions:

1. What are the different ways that Jesus was tortured before being crucified?
2. What did Pilate say about the charges that were made against Jesus?
3. What law did the Jews say that Jesus was guilty of?
    a. Why was that not true for Jesus?
4. When Pilate asked Jesus where He was from, Jesus didn't respond. Pilate then stated He had authority over Jesus to either set Him free or crucify Him. Where did Jesus say that Pilate's authority over Him came from?
5. Who actually wanted Jesus crucified?
    a. Why was this significant?
6. What was written above Jesus' head?
7. What did the soldiers do with Jesus' garments?
    a. Why was this significant?
8. How did Jesus die?
9. What did the soldiers do to Jesus that was different from the other two who were crucified?
    a. Why was that important?
10. Who took the responsibility of burying Jesus' body?

# Day 20: Why Can't I Have a Beer After Work?

I gave my testimony and a short message at a local Christ-based drug and alcohol rehab in February 2022. I was filling in for my friend, who couldn't teach that day. It was only my second time speaking in front of a group of people. I had an hour to speak, but my testimony and message lasted only twenty-one minutes. I asked the group of guys if anyone had any questions or comments.

During my testimony, I told the guys that a relationship with Jesus is the only way out of addiction. One guy spoke up and said, "There has to be another way. I am married, have a good job, my own house, and custody of my kids. Why can't I come home after a long day at work and have a beer to relax?" To be completely honest, I wasn't prepared at the time to answer his question.

*But God.* God had other program participants in the room ready to speak up and help the guy with this question. Four other guys and I were all witnessing to this guy and two others in the room for the last forty minutes. It was a beautiful experience. One guy that we were witnessing to actually rededicated his life to Jesus that day.

Alcohol isn't something I have ever really struggled with. I hadn't thought much about addiction at the time other than overcoming my own video game addiction. Since that day, I have put a lot of thought into all forms of addiction.

If I had the chance again, I would answer his question with a question. Can you come home after work and only have *one* beer? And this question applies to anyone facing addiction or idols that keep them from seeking Jesus. Can you look at social media without scrolling for hours? Can you play a video game for an hour and feel satisfied that you have accomplished enough? Can you watch one episode of your favorite show on Netflix without wanting to watch more?

The answer is *boundaries*. Yesterday, I mentioned that watching TV, playing video games, or looking at social media in and of themselves are not sinful. The sin of idolatry is when any of these things keep you from seeking Jesus daily. Before you decide to reintroduce anything that has been an idol, you have to search your heart and ask yourself some questions.

Why do I feel the need to reintroduce these things into my life? What am I seeking to get from these activities? Is there something I think I can get from these activities that I am not getting from my relationship with Jesus and other people? Am I ready to establish boundaries for these activities?

After my experience with Jesus telling me that I had to stop playing my video games, I stopped playing them completely for about nine months and was seeking Jesus daily. I was searching my heart and getting to know Jesus. I was reading Christian self-help books, those the Holy Spirit led me to read, to help me heal from the damage my idols had caused and the hurt others had caused me.

When I finally decided to reintroduce my idol, video games, into my life, I searched my heart and realized my particular problems. Playing games on my phone was too accessible for me, and playing online games with others was too tempting. I set boundaries for myself. I wouldn't play any game on my phone anymore. I wouldn't play any on-line games anymore. I could only play single-player games that didn't put me in the position of having someone else depending on me.

The other thing I had to do was to ensure that I was still seeking a relationship with Jesus daily. This would help me ensure that I was getting the love I needed from God to fulfill my heart and help me continue to grow my faith in Jesus. What I found out from this surprised me.

When I reintroduced gaming into my life, I didn't have the same desire to play video games that I had before. I enjoyed playing them still, of course. But the enjoyment wasn't exactly the same. I realized I no longer needed to play video games to meet my needs. Jesus was already meeting those needs, and my relationship with Jesus is where my joy came from.

Social media is a more difficult one to address. Many people get their social interactions from social media now. If you have recognized social media as an idol for you that has been keeping you from seeking a relationship with Jesus, I would advise you to search your heart and ask yourself some questions:

- Am I using social media as a replacement for real-life relationships?
- Am I neglecting my relationships with my spouse, children, friends, or family to seek relationships online with people I barely know?
- Why are these people so important to me that I neglect the people who love me?
- Am I not feeling loved by the people who should be loving me?
- Am I using social media as a form of escaping real-world problems?

These are just a few questions you can ask yourself to get to the root of the problem.

There is another form of idolatry that social media can help fuel. That is self-idolatry. Self-idolatry is when people believe they are the center of their own world. Everything revolves around them, and their opinion is the only opinion that matters. They are deciding that they know better than God how to live their lives.

Proverbs 18:2 says, *"A fool does not delight in understanding, but only in revealing his own mind."* We defined *fool* the other day, but I want to remind you again. The word used for *fool* is *kesîl*. A fool is "a person who expects things 'to go his way' even when lazy and irresponsible. He is constantly unrealistic, especially when it serves his selfish purposes. Doing this he brings needless pains by insisting on choices that are ignorant of cause-and-effect relationships. He cherishes ridiculous expectations and disregards physical and moral laws." [1]

Psalms 14:1 says, *"The fool has said in his heart, 'There is no God.'"* This is a question every unbeliever has to ask himself: "Am I being a fool for not believing?" Proverbs 12:15 says, *"The way of a fool is right in his own eyes, but a wise man is he who listens to counsel."* If you believe that only you know the way that is right, ask yourself a few questions.

- How has my life been going up until this point?
- Has life seemed easy, or has life seemed hard?
- Have my choices caused these difficulties for me?

If you truly search your past and answer these questions honestly, you could determine if your problem is self-idolatry.

The good news is that this is a pretty easy fix. All you have to do is accept this truth about yourself and start seeking a relationship with Jesus. Accept that you don't know everything and start seeking the One who does. I believe that self-idolatry was one of my issues. I believed I knew better how to live my life than God did. I can honestly say that my life didn't go very well then.

If you decide to reintroduce yourself to social media, what boundaries could you set to protect yourself? First, you could give yourself set times each day to use social media to keep up with the people you care about online that matter to you. Make sure that before using social media, you have spent time reading the Word and seeking Jesus daily.

Second, commit to avoiding using social media during set family times. For example, my wife would be looking at Facebook, and I would play a video game on my phone when we were supposed to be watching a movie together at home. This made us feel like we weren't important to each other. This wasn't healthy for either of us.

Third, have an accountability partner who helps keep track of how much time you spend on social media. This isn't an easy task, but until you gain the self-control that spiritual maturity brings, you will need help. This person could be your spouse or a friend. You could even set a timer or an alarm for yourself that will go off to ensure you realize how long you have been scrolling.

Last, cell phones have restrictions that can be activated that limit screen time for certain activities. There is nothing wrong with setting limits for yourself to help you realize when it's time to move on to a healthier activity.

Tomorrow, we will address the question, "What do I do now after finishing this devotional?" We will discuss how to continue seeking a relationship with Jesus. And I will offer some suggestions on books I have read that have helped me overcome my personal struggles.

*Before proceeding to the next section, review and ask yourself the self-reflection questions listed in the "How to Use This Devotional" section at the beginning of this book.*

# Day 20 Prayer

Father God, today is day 20 of my fast. I have learned a lot about You, Father. I have learned that You love me. You love me so much that You sent Your Son, Jesus, to die for me. For that, Father, I thank You.

I have also been learning a lot about myself. I have learned that I have been putting my idols of _____ before seeking a relationship with You, Father. Please forgive me for that. As I draw close to the end of this devotional and the time I set aside to fast from my idols to see You, Father, I am asking You to help me make some hard decisions. Father, I need You to show me what I should do. Should I go back to the activities I was fasting from that kept me from seeking You? Or do I need to spend more time away from these activities and draw myself closer to You before I consider introducing these activities back into my life?

Search my heart, Father, and reveal the truth about myself. Am I using these activities to meet the needs that You were always meant to meet for me? Are these activities damaging relationships with the people You have placed in my life? Am I trying to be my own god instead of letting You be my God? These are hard questions for me to face, Father; please be with me as I ask myself these questions. Help me be truly honest with myself. I want to know these truths to start healing my heart and want what You want.

You want to have a relationship with me, Father, and for me to go out to make disciples for You. Father, I love You and thank You for helping me realize that I need You. I ask You all these things in Jesus' Mighty Name, Amen!

# Day 20 Bible Study Questions

Read John chapter 20 and answer the following questions:

1. What did Mary Magdalene find when she came to the tomb Jesus was buried in?
   a. What did she tell Simon and John (the other disciple) that she thought had happened to His body?
2. What did Peter and John do once they heard what Mary said?
   a. What did Simon find when He entered the tomb?
3. As Mary was weeping outside the tomb, who appeared to her?
   a. What did they ask her?
   b. What did Mary say?
4. Who did Mary see next, and who did she think He was?
5. What did Jesus say to Mary to get her to recognize it was Him?
6. What did Jesus tell Mary to do?
7. What did Jesus do for the disciples to help them recognize it was Him?
8. What happened when Jesus breathed on them?
9. Which disciple wasn't there to see Jesus the first time?
   a. What did He say that he needed to see to believe?
10. Why did John write the book?

# Day 21: What Do I Do Now After Finishing this Devotional?

This devotional has been a very structured plan for you to follow. This structure has been to teach you what following Jesus looks like. Another reason for the structure has been to help you fill the free time during the fast. Now that you have almost finished this devotional, what should you do to keep moving forward in your new life with Jesus?

This is the same problem people have after completing rehab. They must figure out how to go out into the world without the structure and not fall back into their old patterns of behavior. Unlike rehab, though, I have been teaching you how to live this new life.

I have told you since day one that you needed to do this program with another person. The purpose of doing this was to teach you how to be a disciple. Discipleship is an essential part of the Christian lifestyle. We need each other to grow and learn about Jesus. If you have done this devotional with another person, you have already established a relationship to move forward with. Keep talking with this person. Keep learning with this person. Keep being accountable to each other.

If this is the first time you have read the Bible, you are not alone. My first fast was the first time I had read the Bible, too. Keep reading. I would suggest starting in the book of Matthew, the first book of the New Testament, and reading at least two chapters every day or as long as the Holy Spirit leads you.

Another option is the find a Bible reading plan that will help guide you into what to read. You could search online or use the YouVersion.com Bible app to find a Bible reading plan to follow. I would also suggest following this reading plan with your partner for accountability. You should still be meeting at least once a week to help each other learn about Jesus.

As you read the Bible daily, continue to search your heart. Pray to God, asking Him to help you continue to apply what you are learning about Him to your daily life. Prayer is very important to God. Reading the Bible is how God speaks to you. Prayer is how you speak to God. That is what a relationship requires, communication with each other.

Jesus said in John 15:7, *"If you abide in Me, and My words abide in you, ask whatever you wish, and it will be done for you."* When Jesus says to abide in Me, He means to read and follow His Word, the Bible. When He says ask whatever you wish, He is talking about praying to Him for His will to be done in your life.

If you started going to church during this devotional, keep going. Find ways to serve other people in your community. Remember what we said that God said was good? Love God first, then love your neighbor. Paul said in Galatians 5:13, *"For you were called to freedom, brethren; only do not turn your freedom into an opportunity for the flesh, but through love serve one another."* This freedom Paul is talking about is the freedom from sin to do God's will. Turning our focus from ourselves to serving others in humility gives life a new perspective.

Paul also said in 1 Thessalonians 1:9-10, *"For they themselves report about us what kind of a reception we had with you, and how you turned to God from idols to serve a living and true God, and to wait for His Son from heaven, whom He raised from the dead, that is Jesus, who rescues us from the wrath to come."* Paul says we are waiting for His Son, Jesus, to return. But while we are waiting, we should be serving others by carrying out the Great Commission.

While you search your heart and pray for God to reveal things to you, look for unresolved areas of hurt or how you have hurt others. One area we haven't discussed in depth yet is forgiveness. We know that Jesus has forgiven us our sins. How do we forgive other people?

Matthew 18:21-35 deals with the issue of forgiveness. I want to focus on verses 21 and 22: *"Then Peter came and said to Him, 'Lord, how often shall my brother sin against me and I forgive him? Up to seven times?' Jesus said to him, 'I do not say to you, up to seven times, but up to seventy times seven.'"* When Jesus told Peter this, He showed Peter how important forgiveness is. But what is forgiveness?

First, let's talk about what forgiveness is not. Forgiveness is not letting people off the hook. It's not forgetting what happened to you. It's not allowing yourself to be constantly hurt by someone. Forgiveness is doing what Jesus modeled for us to do on the cross. It's seeing and thinking about people the way God sees them. Let's look at what Jesus said about forgiveness on the cross.

In Luke 23:33-34, Jesus modeled how we should forgive others. *"When they came to the place called The Skull, there they crucified Him and the criminals, one on the right and the other on the left. But Jesus was saying, 'Father, forgive them; for they do not know what they are doing.'"* They had beaten Jesus, mocked Him, made Him wear a crown of thorns, stripped Him naked, and crucified Him on a wooden cross. [1]

Jesus prayed this prayer right after He was hung on the cross. He knew that His Father loved them even though they sinned against Him. We have to learn to remember to want what God wants. God wants people. When we learn to see people in light of what God wants for them, it becomes easier to offer forgiveness.

Romans 5:8 says, *"But God demonstrates His own love toward us, in that while we were yet sinners, Christ died for us."* God loves us so much that He sent Jesus to die for us while we were sinners, and Jesus loves us so much that He asked for our forgiveness while dying for us. Don't you think we should learn to love people the same way?

Forgiveness is learning to realize that people who are hurting us may be lost. They need us to demonstrate God's forgiveness, even when they may not deserve it. It also keeps us from having resentment in our hearts because you can't truly forgive someone unless you have love for them.

After we forgive someone, we must find a way to heal our hearts. Jesus can do that for us when we ask Him. But sometimes, we need to change our way of thinking to accept that healing. How do we do that?

I can't say what will work for you. But what worked for me was reading Christian self-help books. I will give you a list of books that helped me, along with a brief discussion of each book.

For a book to help someone who may be still struggling with unbelief, the book *Mere Christianity* by C.S. Lewis is a good starting point. Lewis was an atheist who, through questioning morality, became a believer himself. He is a British author, so the book is written in Old English; it took me a while to read it. But Lewis does well in explaining how morality proves God's existence.

Do you struggle with negative thinking? I sure did. The Spirit led me to the book *Crash the Chatterbox* by Steven Furtick. Furtick helps you learn to recognize and reject the negative thoughts Satan tries to put in your mind. It helped me tremendously to change my outlook on life.

In *Slaying the Giants in Your Life*, David Jeremiah covers various topics like fear, worry, doubts, guilt, temptation, and more. He helps you learn how to face these "giants" from a Biblical perspective to have victory over these areas.

*The Bait of Satan* by John Bevere tackles the trap of offense Satan lays for us to try to make us hate each other. Bevere teaches the skill of learning how not to allow others to offend you.

*Victory in Spiritual Warfare* by Tony Evans teaches you to overcome spiritual warfare by putting on the full armor of God. He starts by showing you the devil's schemes to tempt us. He then shows you how to equip the spiritual armor Paul describes in Ephesians 6:13-17. He goes through each type of armor piece by piece so you can engage in spiritual warfare and have victory in Jesus Christ.

The books suggested here are not a requirement but a starting point for finding your healing. The Holy Spirit led me to each one of these books, which spoke to something specific that I was going through at the time. My suggestions are nothing compared to the Holy Spirit that dwells in you. Jesus knows everything about you from the day you were born to the present day. He has seen it all and wants to help you. That's why He sent you the Helper, the Holy Spirit, to guide you.

I hope this book has helped lead you to a closer relationship with Jesus and destroyed the idols keeping you from Him. My last call is for you to stand firm in your faith in Jesus and don't give up. No matter how bad it is, Jesus loves you and wants to help you.

*Before proceeding to the next section, review and ask yourself the self-reflection questions listed in the "How to Use This Devotional" section at the beginning of this book.*

# Day 21 Prayer

Father God, as I start this new journey in my life following You, I need Your help. Help me, through the Holy Spirit You have placed in me, to keep seeking You. Fill me with Your Spirit and lead me to what You want me to do to keep seeking You. Give me someone to go through this journey with me, someone who can help keep me accountable and learn about You with me, someone whom I can help, too. Father, lead me to a church where I can learn how to serve others. Help me, Father, search my heart for any hurt I haven't healed from and show me how to forgive others who have hurt me. Help me learn how to forgive others because You have forgiven Me. Help me to want what You want: people. Give me compassion, kindness, humility, grace, hope, and love to show others so that they can know that I am Yours. If you want me to start reading books to help me learn how to heal, show me which books to read. Father, I want to end by giving you all the glory, honor, and praise that You and only You deserve. You are worthy of my praise, Father. Help me to praise you all day long. Help me to keep You in my heart. I ask these things in Jesus' Mighty Name, Amen.

# Day 21 Bible Study Questions

Read John chapter 21 and answer the following questions:

1. Who were the disciples that Jesus revealed Himself to at the Sea of Galilee?
   a. What were they doing?
2. What did Jesus ask them to do that helped reveal to them who He really was?
3. What did Peter do when he realized it was Jesus?
4. What did Jesus do for them when they came ashore?
5. What question did Jesus ask Simon three times?
   a. Why do you think Jesus asked Simon three times? Hint: think back to John chapter 18.
   b. What did Jesus tell Simon to do each time?
   c. What did Jesus mean by that?
6. What did Jesus tell them they would go through for following Him?

# References

INTRODUCTION
1. Luke 15:11-13
2. John 3:16

DAY 1: HOW DOES THE WORLD DEFINE ADDICTION?
1. Merriam-Webster.com Dictionary, s.v. "addiction," accessed April 26, 2022, https://www.merriam-webster.com/dictionary/addiction.

DAY 2: HOW DOES GOD DEFINE ADDICTION?
1. Merriam-Webster.com Dictionary, s.v. "addiction," accessed April 26, 2022. https://www.merriam-webster.com/dictionary/addiction.
2. Merriam-Webster.com Dictionary, s.v. "inclination," accessed April 26, 2022, https://www.merriam-webster.com/dictionary/inclination.
3. Matthew 22:37
4. H.E.L.P.S. Ministries. 2022. Word study "(SN 2442) ḥāḵâ" accessed April 26, 2022. The Discovery Bible Software. www.discoverybible.com.
5. H.E.L.P.S. Ministries. "(SN 2580) ḥēn"
6. H.E.L.P.S. Ministries. "(SN 7355) rāḥam"
7. Psalms 55:1-3
8. Psalms 3:3

DAY 3: AM I CONSUMING ENTERTAINMENT OR IS ENTERTAINMENT CONSUMING ME?
1. Merriam-Webster.com Dictionary, s.v. "consume," accessed April 27, 2022, https://www.merriam-webster.com/dictionary/consume.
2. Merriam-Webster.com Dictionary, s.v. "entertainment,"

accessed April 27,2022, https://www.merriamwebster.com/dictionary/entertainment.

3. Statista Research Department. 2022. "Daily time spent on social networking by internet users worldwide from 2012 to 2022." Accessed Mar. 31, 2022. www.statista.com/statistics/433871/daily-social-media-usage-worldwide.

4. Gordon, Billi Ph.D. Oct. 20, 2017. "Social Is to Your Brain and Relationships." *Psychology Today.* www.psychologytoday.com/us/blog/obesely-speaking/201710/social-media-is-harmful-your-brain-and-relationships

5. Weinschenk, Susan Ph.D. Sept. 11, 2012. "Why We're All Addicted to Texts, Twitter and Google." *Psychology Today.* www.psychologytoday.com/us/blog/brain-wise/201209/why-were-all-addicted-texts-twitter-and-google.

6. H.E.L.P.S. Ministries. "(SN 3615) kālâ"

7. Exodus 20:3-4

8. H.E.L.P.S. Ministries. "(SN 3684) kesîl"

9. H.E.L.P.S. Ministries. "(SN 60) ebel"

DAY 4: WHAT IS FASTING?

1. H.E.L.P.S. Ministries. "(SN 7563) rāsha'"

2. Deibert, Brannon. Feb. 12, 2019. "What is the meaning of yoke in the Bible? Meaning and importance of Jesus' teaching." www.christianity.com/jesus/life-of-jesus/teaching-and-messages/the-yoke-of-jesus-biblical-meaning-and-importance.html.

3. H.E.L.P.S. Ministries. "(SN 7533) rāṣaṣ"

4. H.E.L.P.S. Ministries. "(SN 5956) 'ālaṃ "

DAY 5: WHO IS GOD?

1. Genesis 1:1

2. Genesis 1:3-5

3. Genesis 1:6-25
4. H.E.L.P.S. Ministries. "(SN 6918) qadosh"
5. Isaiah 30:18
6. H.E.L.P.S. Ministries. "(SN 4243) presbeúō"

DAY 6: WHAT IS SIN?
1. Genesis chapters 1-2
2. Exodus 20: 3-17
3. Romans 3:23
4. Genesis 2:19-23
5. H.E.L.P.S. Ministries. "(SN 4655) skótos"
6. Psalms 69:1-3, 5, 10, 13-18

DAY 7: WHO IS JESUS?
1. John 14:6
2. John 1:1-2
3. John 1:4-9
4. John 1:29
5. John 1:34
6. John 1:38
7. John 2:6-11
8. Matthew 28:18
9. John 3:16-17
10. John 4:10
11. John 4:19
12. John 4:25-26
13. John 4:46-53
14. H.E.L.P.S. Ministries. "(SN 2316) theós"
15. Isaiah 7:14
16. H.E.L.P.S. Ministries. "(SN 5547) Xristós"
17. John 19
18. 1 Corinthians 15: 3-8
19. Acts 1:9-11

DAY 8: WHY DO I NEED JESUS?
1. H.E.L.P.S. Ministries. "(SN 4655) skótos"
2. Revelation 20:11-15
3. H.E.L.P.S. Ministries. "(SN 1067) géenna"
4. H.E.L.P.S. Ministries. "(SN 2805) klauthmós"
5. H.E.L.P.S. Ministries. "(SN 3599) odoús"
6. Revelation 12:7-9
7. H.E.L.P.S. Ministries. "(SN 2851) kolasis"

DAY 9: HOW DO I FOLLOW JESUS?
1. H.E.L.P.S. Ministries. "(SN 5046) nāgaḏ"
2. H.E.L.P.S. Ministries. "(SN 2895) ṭôb̲"
3. H.E.L.P.S. Ministries. "(SN 4941) mishpāṭ"
4. H.E.L.P.S. Ministries. "(SN 2617a) ḥeseḏ"
5. H.E.L.P.S. Ministries. "(SN 430) Ělōhîm"
6. H.E.L.P.S. Ministries. "(SN 1980) halak"
7. H.E.L.P.S. Ministries. "(SN 6800) ṣāna'"
8. Psalms 8

DAY 10: HOW DO I DRAW MYSELF CLOSER TO GOD?
1. H.E.L.P.S. Ministries. "(SN 1785) entolē"
2. John 14:14
3. Psalms 25:4-11

DAY 11: WHO IS THE HOLY SPIRIT?
1. H.E.L.P.S. Ministries. "(SN 3875) paráklētos"
2. H.E.L.P.S. Ministries. "(SN 266) hamartía"
3. H.E.L.P.S. Ministries. "(SN 1343) dikaiosýnē"
4. H.E.L.P.S. Ministries. "(SN 1651) elégxō"

DAY 12: HOW DO I TEACH MY HEART TO WANT WHAT GOD WANTS?
1. H.E.L.P.S. Ministries. "(SN 3820) lēb̲"
2. H.E.L.P.S. Ministries. "(SN 7451b) ra'"

3. Genesis 6:6-9:17
4. Psalms 51:1-17

DAY 13: HOW DO I CIRCUMCISE MY HEART?
1. H.E.L.P.S. Ministries. "(SN 4135) mûl"
2. Archer, Gleason. 1982. *Encyclopedia of Bible Difficulties.*
   *Zondervan. 93.*
3. Psalms 69:32-33

DAY 14: WHAT IS LOVE?
1. John 3:16
2. H.E.L.P.S. Ministries. "(SN 25) agapáō"
3. H.E.L.P.S. Ministries. "(SN 4624) skandalízō"

DAY 15: HOW DO I RENEW MY MIND?
1. H.E.L.P.S. Ministries. "(SN 5252) hyperphronéō"
2. H.E.L.P.S. Ministries. "(SN 3339) metamorphóō"
3. H.E.L.P.S. Ministries. "(SN 4102) pístis"
4. H.E.L.P.S. Ministries. "(SN 1939) epithymía"

DAY 17: HOW DO I HELP OTHERS BEAR SPIRITUAL FRUIT?
1. H.E.L.P.S. Ministries. "(SN 2590) karpós"
2. Psalms 51:10-17

DAY 18: WHAT IS A DISCIPLE?
1. H.E.L.P.S. Ministries. "(SN 2377) ḥāzôn"
2. H.E.L.P.S. Ministries. "(SN 6544a) para"
3. H.E.L.P.S. Ministries. "(SN 4198) poreúomai"
4. H.E.L.P.S. Ministries. "(SN 3100) mathēteúō"

DAY 19: WHAT IF I FALL BACK INTO TEMPTATION?
1. H.E.L.P.S. Ministries. "(SN 341) anakainóō"
2. H.E.L.P.S. Ministries. "(SN 38) hagiasmós"
3. H.E.L.P.S. Ministries. "(SN 4337) proséxō"

4. Matthew 18:7-9

DAY 20: WHY CAN'T I HAVE A BEER AFTER WORK?
1. H.E.L.P.S. Ministries. "(SN 3684) kesîl"

DAY 21: WHAT DO I DO NOW AFTER FINISHING THIS
DEVOTIONAL?
1. Matthew 27:27-44

# Acknowledgments

Without the influence of many people during my life, this book would have never been written. I want to take a few minutes to thank the people who have been an integral part of my Christian walk and the process of getting this book written.

First, I want to give all the glory to God. Thank you, Jesus, for loving us enough to die for us so that we could be saved and experience a relationship with Your Father that words can never fully express. Thank you, Lord, for being patient during my time of idolatry and never giving up on me. Thank you, Lord, for sending people into my life that helped guide me to You, the One I needed to overcome my idolatry. Thank you, Lord, for giving me the opportunity to meet Jesus personally through my time of fasting. Thank you, Lord, for sending people into my life that saw something in me that I didn't see in myself. Thank you, Jesus, for allowing me to be a part of Your Kingdom by including me in Your story of how You helped me to overcome my idolatry by fasting and seeking You. Thank you, Holy Spirit, for speaking to me and guiding my hand during this process of telling Your story in a way that gives You the glory that only You deserve.

Aleah Ozbirn, thank you for confronting me with the truth of how my video game idolatry was affecting our marriage negatively. Thank you for being patient with me for eight years during my time of idolatry, giving me time to change before you had to make the difficult decision to leave the marriage. Thank you for the sacrifices you made for our family during the time my idolatry was keeping me from fulfilling my responsibilities. God used you in my life to help me realize that video games were an idol to me and for that I am eternally grateful.

Pastor Terry Ledbetter, thank you for challenging me to participate in a church-wide fast in January of 2018. Thank you for explaining to me that fasting isn't only about food but about abstaining from anything that could be keeping me from seeking a relationship with Jesus. This fast led me to a personal encounter with Jesus. This encounter with Jesus led me to destroy my idols and obtain eternal salvation. Without your being led by the Holy Spirit to call for a church-wide fast, I would never have overcome my idolatry and never had the testimony that led me to writing this book.

Brad and Selena Davis, thank you both for being a light in the darkness for me when I was struggling in my idolatry. You both listened to me talk about the problems that my idolatry was causing me and gave me Godly advice that I rarely followed. You both showed great patience and Godly love for me that I had never been shown before. The example you both modeled for me helped lead me closer to Jesus. For these reasons, I will never forget the positive effect you both had on my life.

Bill and Angela Sloan, thank you both for loving me like your own children. Thank you for pouring God's love into me and sitting and talking with me for hours about Jesus. The influence you made on my walk with God means the world to me.

Sharon Bowen, thank you, Mom, for loving me and doing your very best to take care of me. Thank you for raising me to love other people and always praying for me when I wasn't living a Godly life. God used your prayers to soften my heart so that I could be reconciled to Him. I love you.

Danny Ozbirn, thank you, Dad, for always taking care of me, for fighting for my safety when I was abused, and helping me financially whenever I was struggling. Thank you for teaching me how to be a hard worker and always encouraging me to be my very best. I love you.

Harold Patterson, thank you for walking up to me one day after service, handing me your card, and inviting me to coffee. From the day we met, you have poured your life into me and helped me to grow spiritually in a way I would have never imagined possible. I will spend the rest of my life making sure the leadership and training you have demonstrated on how to be a disciple of Jesus will impact the kingdom of God to the ends of the earth until the end of time. I will never be able to repay you for how much you have blessed me. May you shine with the glory of the host of heaven when Jesus returns to set up His kingdom on earth.

Chris Payne, thank you for showing me what it looks like to have passion for helping people who are struggling in life by telling them, "There is A WAY OUT and that way out is Jesus." You helped me to see that one person who is working alongside the Holy Spirit can made a huge difference in people's lives. Thank you for encouraging me to share my testimony with others. Thank you for sharing my testimony with someone who you knew would use it to bring God glory. You were the spark that started this process, and for that, I am grateful.

Opie Hurst, thank you for being humble enough to reach out to me after hearing my testimony to get help when you didn't have the answers yourself. Thank you for allowing the Holy Spirit to lead you to me. Thank you for asking me the question, "How do I help other people realize they have an addiction?" While I didn't know the answer to the question at the time, God did, and He knew he could use my testimony to answer your question as well as bring Him the glory that He deserves. Thank you for working alongside the Holy Spirit to lead me to the idea of writing this book. The impact you have made on my life will be used by God to reach people throughout the world. I am grateful to call you a brother in Christ.

www.ingramcontent.com/pod-product-compliance
Lightning Source LLC
Chambersburg PA
CBHW021633120626
46545CB00002B/517